C000184842

Veggin' out

If this book has made it to your kitchen
a BIG THANK YOU!

From my kitchen to yours,
from my table to yours,
from my plate to yours,
from my fork to yours...

With gratitude and love,

@JUSTVEGGINGJAZ

Ingredients in this Book

Introduction

Welcome to my book, beautiful people! I'm Jaz, a certified plant-based nutritionist and foodie with a passion for creative plant-based cooking and a focus on living life more naturally and sustainably. I'm a strong believer in the studies that show how reducing, or even better removing, meat and processed foods from your diet can decrease disease, boost your health and improve our earth's health all at the same time. However, I would like to point out that I have not written this book to convince people that they should be living a meat-free lifestyle, but more to highlight all the benefits that come with eating more plants.

There's something in this book for everyone, whether you are a fully-fledged vegetarian (also known throughout this book as a 'veggie' or 'veggo') like me, a vegan or still on the fence. For those who are looking to transition, please treat it as a lifestyle rather than a diet and know that I am not a doctor or qualified dietitian, so do consult one or both before making any drastic changes to your diet.

It has taken me years to get a grip on my health and to reap the full benefits of a plant-based lifestyle, so my wish is for this book to guide you through this journey, making it a much easier one for you than it was for me by sharing my personal experience and professional knowledge. This includes my learnings, lessons, facts about the positive impacts of plants and how I vegetated towards veggies, because here's the thing: it ain't all sunshine and pretty rainbow poké bowls. Through my recipes, I will also show you how to mimic meat with veggies, fruits, nuts, seeds, and legumes so you can still enjoy tasty and fulfilling roasts, steaks and hearty pies... just without the cow, lamb, chicken, pig or Skippy the kangaroo!

These recipes have been inspired by my childhood and my travels, then created with the aim of mimicking the aesthetic and texture of meat, so it feels like you are eating the "real" (meaty) thing. My 100 delicious meat-free ideas range from finger-licking party foods that will keep your friends and family hanging around, to morning meals that help break the fast. And who said you can't make friends with salad? If you're feeling a little saucy or perhaps a bit naughty, there happens to be a few recipes in here for that too!

I am absolutely over the moon to have the opportunity to share these with you. I hope you enjoy cooking and eating them as much as I did creating them. Happy learning, happy cooking. Let's get our veg on! But first, I'm going to get a little raw...

The Raw Me

When I was a sprout...

I grew up in a low socioeconomic household, and my parents did their best within their means to feed us healthy, homemade meals cooked from scratch when they could. Our family followed the typical Australian diet of 'meat and three veg' which meant roasts every Sunday, bangers and mash, chicken snitty (schnitzel), burgers (with the lot), meat pies, Chiko Rolls (an Aussie savoury snack) and fish 'n' chips, just to name a few. Oh, and how could I forget Dad's delicious spaghetti bolognese with a special secret ingredient, which years later I learnt was Skippy the kangaroo... thanks Dad.

We rarely had take-out, but on fortnightly occasions when payday came around we were treated to a dine-in experience at the world-famous Restaurant McDonald's. Oh boy, did our Happy Meals make us kids happy, especially when complemented by a cool toy! In general, soft drinks were a big NO, so it was either water, cordial or milk to drink. To cure our sweet tooth, when we asked for a lolly the response we got was an apple, orange or peach: whatever fruit was in reach. As a treat, we baked homemade cakes or cookies alongside Mum. For dessert, we were allowed frozen yoghurt fruit cups or Neapolitan ice cream. I only liked the strawberry flavour and my brother only liked the chocolate; vanilla was simply just "too vanilla" for us kids.

I was young, dumb, and full of junk.

From my childhood through to my adolescent years, funnily enough, I was always surrounded by produce and quite competent at cooking. Moving out at the young age of 15 with no support meant I really had no other choice but to learn how to cook and get a job to come up with the weekly rent. However, I had a different notion of cooking back then and saw it as survival or a chore rather than something I enjoyed.

The first ever job I landed was at a small but very popular family-owned fruit and vegetable shop in my hometown of Newcastle, Australia. I juggled my studies, part-time work and trying to be an independent teenager, so instead of attending beach raves and parties full of underage drinking and getting up to no good, my weekends consisted of packing fruit and vegetables on shelves. Mind you, I did quite enjoy the job. After I completed my studies, having no idea what I wanted to do with my life or career, I was employed full-time as a produce and deli assistant by my local supermarket.

As a busy teenager without much moral support, I became lazy and took advantage of being able to eat whatever I wanted, whenever I wanted. I also had the freedom of finally being able to eat all the things I could not afford before. Wasn't that a recipe for disaster! I was having a field day with junk food. My weekly shopping trolley consisted of 70% processed or junk food and 30% fruit and veg. I had created the worst eating habits and from that I created the biggest sweet tooth and a vicious cycle of constant cravings for fast foods.

I even became addicted to coke... Coca Cola, that is. Not the other kind! I was buying bottles and cans in packs of 24 for the week, and stocking up whenever it was on sale. I drank it with every meal apart from breakfast, and simply to quench my thirst. Coca Cola would have made me an ambassador if they knew how much I was consuming! That is a hard pill to swallow these days, but hey, as long as we live and learn right? Now I understand why my parents were so strict about soft drinks and confectionery when I was a kid; it wasn't just because we were poor after all. In my parent's famous last words: "don't say we didn't tell you so, kiddo!"

Look deep into nature and you will understand everything better

Vegetating Towards Veggies

Your environment

The first and most important thing to nail in the transition to a plant-based lifestyle is your environment. What I have personally experienced the hard way is that unhealthy eating habits are accompanied by unhealthy thoughts and an unhealthy appearance, along with many other health issues. It is all connected. And so the moment I changed my environment, my relationship with food changed too. By this time, I was 21 and had started a new career path then separated from my long-term teenage love, so I had a new home life and a new work life. This was a rebirth for my health: a new beginning, a new me!

> the moment I changed my environment, my relationship with food changed too

Before I knew it, I had also broken my addiction to Coca Cola. I established a love-hate relationship with water and adopted healthy eating, or so I thought, and only treated myself on occasion. At this point, I was still eating meat but had got rid of the processed foods and junk from my diet. Just by making that small change to my daily eating habits, I noticed such a difference in my mood, mindset and figure. Gradually, the sugar cravings started to fade. It was not easy, but with enough self-discipline you can get there.

They say it takes 21 days to break a habit, and approximately 66 days to create a new one. And heck, did I have some challenges... one in particular springs to mind when I was 23 and, after working my butt off, had just bought my first property. It was a cute little apartment with the big M as my neighbour. Yep, I was close enough to McDonald's for my balcony to have a view of the drive-thru and if I listened in, I could hear people ordering their meals! Oh, and did I mention that I could also smell the food. It was literally calling my name, it was that close. Bloody Ronald!

On the upside, I now had my own space and having a brand-new kitchen in my own little place got me all excited to start researching nourishing, wholesome recipes. I would look forward to the mornings and evenings and on weekends, I would find myself dancing in the kitchen, music up, wine in one hand, spoon in the other, apron on, cooking up a storm and busting moves while waiting for the oven timer to go off. This was my newfound creative outlet and the time when my real love for cooking emerged.

The pinnacle of my path

Around the same time that I discovered my profound love for food, I also was lucky enough to find my mentor and it so happened that he was a pescatarian. If you stay with me, I touch on the pescatarian diet later in the book. I believe there is some sort of truth in the saying 'you are the people you hang around with'. I was intrigued to learn that he had adopted the pescatarian lifestyle and had stuck to it for so many years, especially being a true blue, healthy, athletic Aussie bloke. I thought well heck, being pescatarian must be good so I'm going to give this a whirl! This was the pinnacle of finding my path to a plant-based life.

When I initially adopted this way of eating, I had no idea what I was doing, but after soaking up all the knowledge that was passed on by my mentor and putting it into practice, I just knew that I had to cut out meat and chicken and limit my intake of seafood for the long haul. This approach made me feel good, tasted good and kept me full, and so the pescatarian diet began. Easy peasy... or so I had thought!

The hurdles

You start off with good intentions, then BAM! Someone orders me a Big Mac: "yes, I would like fries with that." You're having a pub feed with friends and get sucked into ordering a chicken snitty: "extra gravy, thanks." You're invited to a barbecue and the smell makes you cave for a sausage sanga: "pass the tomato sauce, would ya?" Change sure as hell doesn't come easy in any context, especially when you make health decisions, and it isn't necessarily about simply flipping the switch. I like to look at change as a process: hard at first, messy in the middle but gorgeous at the end! Some of the initial obstacles that I had to overcome were knowing how to keep my iron and protein levels right; the guilt of being 'too difficult' when eating with family and friends; and of course the cravings... oh, the barbecues tested me every friggin time!

These are just some examples of obstacles that may or may not seem familiar. I am sure you will have a list of your own personal hurdles that you have faced or are yet to face during the early stages of transitioning. It could be that your homelife makes it difficult; you may have a stubborn partner who insists they need their meat-based protein and therefore you find it too time-consuming and costly to cook and serve up two separate meals. Or another goodie: your nearest and dearest repeatedly tell you they are concerned that you are not getting enough iron... thanks guys, but Doc says if I keep eating spinach like Popeye my iron levels will be just fine!

A couple of months went by and I was no longer interested in a big juicy medium rare steak lathered in creamy sauce, but then the next wave of obstacles hit. You know, the messy middle. There is no denying that this way of eating opens up lengthy controversial conversations, which most of the time end in debate and/or judgement. It's important to remember that you should never take advice from people who have not done it, and instead do your own research. Otherwise, you may just spiral back into old eating habits and find yourself locking your jaws around some lovely fatty lamb chops!

As for the gorgeous end, I don't think there ever is an end when it comes to your health and eating habits, as there's always room to improve when seeking that higher self. But look for the lessons in the messy middle, because with enough persistence anything is achievable. I went from eating Skippy the kangaroo to basically living off spinach, and it's the best I've ever felt!

> "I like to look at change as a process. Hard at first, messy in the middle but gorgeous at the end!"

First comes salt, then comes pepper

This is my way of saying that when you focus on the good, the good gets better. Now that I had got a grip on the basics, I thought to myself: what comes next, Jaz? Throughout my life I have found that when something genuinely interests me, I find it essential to research and feed my brain with knowledge on that certain topic. It wasn't school that educated me as I was hardly there! But that's a story for another time. It has always been about books and my personal research. So I turned to books, then to further study of nutrition to learn about the different eating styles and the benefits that come with each one.

The Transition

Different types of plant-based diets

This is a big part of why I wrote this book. Even though plant-based eating is becoming more and more popular, I find that what is often not talked about or understood are the various types of diets, and the many options and alternatives people have.

VEGETARIAN

There are three kinds of vegetarians:
Lacto – Consume dairy products like yoghurt, milk and cheese but do not consume eggs, meat or fish.
Ovo – Do not consume dairy, meat or fish but do consume egg products.
Lacto-ovo – Consume dairy products and eggs but do not consume fish or meat.

VEGAN

Vegan is the strictest diet of them all. They do not consume meat, fish, poultry, dairy or eggs. Some vegans still use honey, but many will not as it is an animal product. Instead, they will substitute honey with maple syrup or rice malt.

PESCATARIAN

In this diet, people will tend to eat fish products. They may also use eggs and dairy products from time to time. They do not consume meat and poultry.

POLLOTARIAN

In this diet, people will tend to eat poultry and eggs but not meat or fish. They may or may not consume dairy products.

FLEXITARIAN

In this diet, people are mostly vegetarian but will include meat infrequently, perhaps once or twice a week.

Step by step guides

1 The Slow Transition

If you are coming from a meat-based diet, also known as omnivorous, I would first and foremost suggest transitioning by following the five-step guide below. I feel the slower the process is, the more effective it will be and the more likely it is to be long-term. I wish I had known of these steps back when I first transitioned. It's important to start by adding more nuts, seeds, tofu, beans, legumes and wholegrains first, before cutting out any meats.

Step 1: Flexitarian – Consuming meat, poultry, seafood and animal by-products infrequently, only once or twice a week.

Step 2: Pollotarian – Consuming only poultry, seafood and animal by-products once or twice a week to replace other meat.

Step 3: Pescatarian – Consuming only seafood and animal by-products once or twice a week to replace poultry and meat.

Step 4: Vegetarian – Cutting out all meat, poultry and seafood but may still include animal by-products such as dairy, eggs and honey.

Step 5: Vegan – Cutting out all meat, poultry and seafood, including any by-products from an animal such as dairy, eggs and honey.

2 The Gradual Transition

Depending on the type of plant-based diet you wish to adopt, you can also choose a gradual transition by following these steps.

Step 1 – Again, start by adding more nuts, seeds, tofu, beans, legumes and wholegrains to your diet before cutting out any meats.

Step 2 – Swap dairy products such as cow's milk for non-dairy alternatives like oat milk, soya milk, coconut or nut milks and plant-based spreads. This is also a good stage to remove any meats that you would not normally consume regularly.

Step 3 – Gradually cut down the rest of your meat intake, including animal by-products, from your least favourite to most.

Step 4 – Now replace any remaining meat or animal by-products with meat alternatives or similar substitutes.

3 The Fast Transition

Perhaps if you are more eager and feel you can be disciplined enough, you can follow these steps for a fast-paced transition. This is more suitable for those who are aiming to adopt a vegan diet as opposed to the other plant-based diets.

Step 1 – Introduce alternatives and add meat substitutes such as plant proteins like tofu, tempeh and seitan. Switch to non-dairy products such as nut milks and dairy-free cheeses, and honey substitutes such as rice malt or maple syrup.

Step 2 – Now cut out all meat, poultry and seafood, including any animal by-products such as dairy, eggs and honey. Include nuts, seeds, tofu, beans, legumes and wholegrains in your diet.

Savvy Kitchen

There's a lot to consider when deciding what food you put on your plate. Even if you are already a vegetarian looking to become vegan, you may run the risk of nutritional deficiencies if you do not balance the diet or prepare properly. Here are some key kitchen pointers to start with.

Anti-nutrients

Plant-based diets are filled with plenty of nutrients and minerals, sometimes more than we need. But what is not talked about so much are the anti-nutrients, which can prevent absorption of certain nutrients and minerals due to the anti-nutrient compounds found in certain food sources. These anti-nutrients are no friend but are not considered harmful, provided you follow a balanced diet.

Phytic Acid (phytate) – Found in seeds, grains and legumes. This reduces the body's mineral absorption if not prepared properly.

Tannins – Found in certain fruits, vegetables, and legumes. An antioxidant that may impair digestion of some nutrients.

Lectins – Found in all edible plants, especially in seeds, legumes and grains. Lectins interfere with absorption of nutrients.

Protease Inhibitors – Found in most edible plants, including legumes and grains. They can interfere with protein digestion.

Calcium Oxalate – Found in many vegetables, mostly in leafy greens, fruit and nuts. They can prevent the absorption of calcium.

These anti-nutrients can be easily avoided and eliminated, provided you do the proper preparation to get the best out of your food.

Proper preparation

It's not a joke, you should soak! In order to reap the rewards of plant-based foods, it's important you get the preparation right. This is because anti-nutrient compounds are mostly found in vegetables, fruits, nuts, seeds, legumes and grains.

For nuts, seeds, legumes and grains

There are a few different methods of removing anti-nutrients: soaking, cooking, sprouting and baking. For less labour-intensive preparation, you can purchase activated or sprouted foods from a wholefoods store, but this tends to be more expensive. By following methods for proper preparation you will also benefit from better digestion and more flavoursome ingredients.

For fruits and vegetables

Give your fruits and vegetables a bath before storing them away after purchase. I invest in a natural veggie wash for my fruits and vegetables as this removes farm chemicals, waxes, surface grime and insects, and it keeps your produce fresher for longer.

Supplements to consider

If you prepare your food properly by taking the necessary steps to remove anti-nutrients, farm chemicals, waxes and unwanted bacteria, you will get the best from your produce. However, due to industrial farming practices, half of the topsoil on the planet has been depleted and has lost most of its mineral content. In addition to soil depletion, more produce is being treated with pesticides, which can add to nutrient loss regardless of how much you nurture them from farm to fridge. This is why you should consider supplementing your diet with certain vitamins and minerals to ensure you are covering all bases for optimal health. These vitamins and minerals can be hard to fit in day to day in a plant-based diet, because there are few reliable sources.

Vitamin B12 – Found in fortified foods, certain non-dairy milks and nutritional yeast flakes.

Vitamin D – For a pescatarian diet it is not essential to take this supplement. However, for vegetarians and vegans it is only found in mushrooms, eggs, tofu and certain fortified foods.

Vitamin K2 – Found in green leafy vegetables or fermented dairy and soy.

Iron – Found in green leafy vegetables, sea vegetables, seeds, nuts, legumes and beans.

Zinc – Found in potatoes, beans, legumes, nuts and seeds.

Omega-3 Fatty Acids – For a pescatarian diet it is not essential to take this supplement. However, for vegetarians and vegans it is recommended.

Protein – Plant protein is the healthiest form of protein. However, some sources of plant foods have lower percentages than animal protein. Plant-based protein powders are ideal for supplementing a varied and balanced diet. Nevertheless, if you are eating a healthy and balanced meat-free diet there is generally no need to add supplementary protein.

Positive Impacts Behind Plants

There are many reasons why people follow plant-based diets. Some of the most common are health, ethics, economics and religion. Everybody's reason will be different and may change over time. My initial reason was to gain control of my health, but it has evolved since then.

My personal positive impacts

Both physically and mentally, I have never been better and I feel as though it's improving with age too. Previously, I had always struggled to maintain my weight throughout my life but nowadays that has become so much easier. Not only have my wellbeing and finances been impacted positively, but my immunity is stronger too. I cannot recall the last time I had to use a tissue for my issue, and I was one to fall sick with the common cold and flu regularly.

Eating a plant-based diet is not only good for our own health, but also for our earth's health. It's no secret that factory farming is one of the biggest causes of pollution on a global scale. I really had no idea how much of an impact an animal-based diet has on our environment. It is quite shocking when you read the facts! No judgement; I used to have a rump steak on my plate at least twice a week. But it is a good feeling to know that nowadays I am doing my tiny little part to protect our beautiful world.

To eat more sustainably is one thing, but to actually live sustainably is even more impactful. Why eat as close to nature as possible but still use everyday products on and in your body that are full of hidden nasty chemicals and preservatives such as parabens and aluminium? My wellbeing has changed drastically since swapping to 100% natural products in my everyday life, alongside a plant-based diet, from personal care to kitchen, bathroom and laundry products. These are all better for yourself and the environment. Remember, we only have one planet and one body so treat them both the best you can!

Another nice little benefit is more money in your pocket. Pre-plant-based eating, I had always assumed it was just too expensive to eat well. But after busting this myth I now realise that you can't put a price on your health, and I have in fact saved so much money by not purchasing meat, particularly because the higher the quality, the higher the cost. The price of my grocery shopping has more than halved and believe me, I eat a lot for a single person: I'm a little piglet! It's all because the produce I'm buying now is very affordable and really versatile.

Disease protection benefits

Studies have shown that a plant-based diet can prevent, reduce and sometimes even reverse certain diseases. Here's a brief guide to the health benefits of different fruits and vegetables according to their colour:

GREEN – Eye health, lung health, liver health and gum health

YELLOW/ORANGE – Reducing inflammation, skin health, immunity, eye health

RED – Reducing inflammation, heart health, cancer prevention, urinary health

PURPLE/BLUE – Immunity, brain health, bone health, skin health

Living the fast life, without the fast food

I now live in the big smoke: London. And it's true when they say the pace of life is faster here. From home to tube station to work, then work to tube station (and sometimes a sneaky stop off at the local bar) to home again and repeat, right through from Monday to Friday. Because we now live in a world where everything has been made quick, easy, and processed (quite like the life I have just described) it's all been made way too easy for us to slip into habits like grabbing food on the go rather than eating a wholesome breakfast at home to start the day, or overindulging by dining out because who the heck likes doing dishes? If you find them, send them my way, would ya!

We tend to look at home cooking as an inconvenience in our busy lives, so in order for us to gain a few extra hours back, we spend money on ready-made meals, have someone cook for us or, even worse, pay someone to deliver it to our door. Don't get me wrong; it's rather nice on occasion, but we unconsciously take advantage of how easy these shortcuts are. We have this mentality that by making these choices, we earn precious time back... but is it really worth it? You still don't know how your food is being made or what ingredients are being used, and you're burning holes in your pocket at the same time. Your nutrition is also probably taking a beating because the food isn't always high quality.

I know, life's not perfect and nobody is. Takeaways and dining out are enjoyable and fine for the odd occasion, as long as we acknowledge when it's time to get back into the kitchen and resume our planned routine, in order to avoid slipping into those naughty habits too often. Just keep in mind that you only have two homes: the first and most important one is your body, mind and soul which needs good healthy food to fuel it. Your second home is earth, which needs us to play a part in looking after the environment so that it can continue looking after us.

I followed my heart and it led me to the fridge

Plant Pantry

"What the heck is nutritional yeast? No way, rice malt really tastes like honey? Tahini... never heard of it!" These are just a few of the ingredients that originally I had no idea even existed, but nowadays they have a permanent home in my pantry and I cannot live without them.

Initially, if you decide not to transition to a plant-based diet slowly and just go for it, it can be an expensive visit to the shops to get set up. Once you have stocked your pantry though, all you will be buying regularly is fresh produce, so in the long run it usually works out cheaper. In my world that means more cash money for this honey to spend on quality coffee and wine!

Most of these ingredients are also really versatile and come with long use-by dates. Hopefully these will make great substitutes for the things that may be rotting in your fridge or growing mould in your pantry right now, which usually get tossed out half-used or, even worse, not opened to begin with. You can make almost anything edible with them. You name it, you can make it finger-licking good!

Here are my key ingredients and smart swaps for a healthy and delicious plant-based pantry:

FOR FLAVOUR

Herbs and spices (ground and fresh)
Nutritional yeast flakes
Liquid smoke
Soy sauce (or tamari, which is wheat-free soy sauce)
Vegetable stock
Sea salt
Cracked black pepper
Raw honey
Pure maple syrup
Vanilla extract
Miso paste
Harissa paste
Apple cider vinegar

FOR TEXTURE

Nuts
Seeds
Grains
Dried fruits
Cornflour
Vital wheat gluten
Agar agar
Beans
Legumes

SMART SWAPS

Everyday Choices

Oils > Olive oil, coconut oil and vegetable oil

Sweeteners > Raw honey, pure maple syrup, coconut sugar or vanilla extract

White bread > Wholemeal or wholegrain bread (see page 174 for my Seeded Spelt Bread recipe)

Milk chocolate > 70% cocoa (or higher) dark chocolate

Caged eggs > Free-range eggs

Table salt > Sea salt

MIMICKING MEAT

Why not ditch the meat and dish up more plants? You will be amazed at how easy it is to mimic meat with plant-based alternatives. Here are some of my favourite ways to do so:

Pulled pork > Jackfruit (see page 100 for my Pulled Jackfruit Burgers recipe)

Chicken > Tofu, chickpeas, cauliflower, jackfruit, oyster mushrooms or seitan (see page 119 for my Seared Seitan and page 120 for my Southern Fried Seitan recipes)

Ground/minced beef > Lentils, black beans, red kidney beans or cauliflower mince (see page 114 for my Cauliflower Mince recipe)

Beef steaks > Portobello mushrooms, cauliflower or seitan (see page 98 for my Mistaken Steak recipe)

Beef burger patties > Portobello mushrooms, beetroot and lentils (see page 88 for my Beet It 'With The Lot' Burger recipe) or aubergine (see page 130 for my Battered Aubergine recipe)

Fish > Tofu (see page 106 for my Fillet-No-Fish recipe)

Bacon > Tempeh, coconut or rice paper vegan 'bacon' (see page 186 for my recipes)

NON-DAIRY IDEAS

Lactose intolerance is a common digestive problem where the body is unable to digest lactose, a type of sugar mainly found in milk and dairy products. If you are like me and done with most dairy, here are some alternatives that are just as tasty and lighter.

Cow's milk > Oat milk, soya milk or any nut milk

Butter/margarine > Nut butter or plant-based butter (made from vegetable oils)

Cream, soured cream, whipped cream or yoghurt > Coconut yoghurt, coconut milk, coconut cream

Cheesy dips or sauces > Tahini, hummus (see page 178 for my recipes) or sauces flavoured with nutritional yeast (see page 165 for my Cheesy Sauce recipe)

Parmesan cheese > Nutritional yeast flakes

Ice cream > Frozen yoghurt (see page 156 for my Frozen Yoghurt Cups recipe)

A Note On The Recipes

For my fellow Aussies out there, here are some swaps I've used throughout the book where British English has different names for common ingredients:

British | Australian

aubergines = eggplants
bell peppers = capsicums
bicarbonate of soda = baking soda
coriander = cilantro
cornflour = cornstarch
courgettes = zucchini
plain flour = all-purpose flour
squash = pumpkin
tin/tinned = can/canned (such as 1 tin of chickpeas or tinned tomatoes)
tomato purée = tomato paste

I measure everything in cups, teaspoons and tablespoons when I cook or bake, but we've provided approximate conversions in grams and millilitres to help those of you who aren't familiar with cup measures. It's important to note that I use the standard Australian (also known as metric) cup which is equivalent to 250ml of water. Because cups are a volume rather than a weight measurement, the conversions you'll see in the recipes differ according to that particular ingredient. For example, flour is lighter than water so 1 cup of plain flour equals approximately 150g.

As for kitchen equipment, the items I have found most useful and that I cannot live without are a quality blender and/or food processor. I would highly suggest investing in one or both. Mine gets a workout at least once a day!

Recipes to eat like a Veggie

Break the Fast

Salads, Soups, Wraps & Bowls

Mimicking Meat

Party with Plants

Something Naughty

Saucy

Make it from Scratch

Break the Fast

SERVES 1 | VEGAN

Coffee & Banana Smoothie

Smoothies are always a great way to start the day. I used to have a banana smoothie and a coffee for breakfast but decided to combine the two, and it is a banger!

What you need

1 frozen banana

1 shot of coffee

1 pitted date

½ cup (125ml) oat milk

½ cup (125ml) water

3-4 ice cubes

Pinch of salt

Pinch of ground cinnamon

2 tbsp chocolate protein powder

Here's how

1. Add all the ingredients to a blender and blitz until smooth. Top with an extra sprinkle of cinnamon if you like.

SERVES 8 | VEGAN

Breakfast Cookies

These cookies are super simple and healthy. No flour, sugar or dairy is needed here; just a couple of ripe bananas will do the trick.

What you need

2 ripe bananas

1 cup (100g) rolled oats

1 tsp ground cinnamon

Here's how

1. Preheat the oven to 170°c. Peel the bananas then mash them together in a mixing bowl until smooth. Pour in the oats and cinnamon and stir until well combined.
2. Now spoon the mixture into cookie-shaped mounds on a silicone baking mat or lined baking tray (it's really important to line the baking tray as these will stick). Use your fingers to make the edges a little smoother and rounder so they bake evenly.
3. Bake the cookies in the preheated oven for 15 minutes, but keep an eye on them as they may cook quicker or need longer depending on how big or small you make them.
4. Remove from the oven and allow to cool slightly before eating.

Oat Bowls

Oats are such a versatile base and generally go well with any topping, so get creative with fruits, spices, nuts and syrups. You will be amazed by some of the flavours you can come up with!

SERVES 1 | VEGETARIAN

Blueberry, Banana & Honey

What you need

1 cup (100g) rolled oats
375ml oat milk or water
1 banana, sliced
½ punnet (75g) blueberries
¼ cup (40g) dried cranberries
¼ cup (30g) flaked almonds
1 tbsp honey

Here's how

1. In a saucepan over a medium heat, combine the oats and oat milk or water. Bring to the boil then simmer for about 8 minutes or until the oats appear soft.
2. Decant the warm oat mixture into a breakfast bowl. Top with the sliced banana, blueberries, cranberries and flaked almonds, then drizzle over the honey.

SERVES 1 | VEGAN

Apple, Maple & Cinnamon

What you need

1 apple
1 cup (100g) rolled oats
375ml oat milk or water
¼ cup (40g) dried mixed fruit
¼ cup (30g) flaked almonds
1 tbsp maple syrup
1 tsp ground cinnamon

Here's how

1. Slice the apple into bite-size pieces and cook gently in a saucepan over a medium heat. Once softened and slightly browned, set aside in a small bowl.
2. Put the oats and oat milk or water into the same saucepan and bring to the boil, then simmer for about 8 minutes or until the oats appear soft.
3. Decant the warm oat mixture into a breakfast bowl. Top with the cooked apple, dried fruit and flaked almonds. Drizzle over the maple syrup and dust with the cinnamon.

SERVES 8 | VEGETARIAN

Flourless Smoothie Muffins

Flourless, fluffy and flavoursome. These muffins are full of fruit and only contain unrefined sugar in the form of honey so they won't weigh you down.

What you need

3 tbsp coconut oil

2 eggs

2 bananas, peeled

2 cups (200g) rolled oats

1 punnet (150g) blueberries

½ cup (100g) honey

65ml oat milk

½ tbsp pure vanilla extract

1½ tsp apple cider vinegar

1 tsp ground cinnamon

1 tsp baking soda

¼ tsp sea salt

Here's how

1. Preheat the oven to 180°c and line a muffin tin with paper cases. Melt the coconut oil in a small pan over a low heat, but do not let it bubble as it will taste burnt.
2. Combine the melted coconut oil with all the other ingredients in a food processor, blending until the batter has a smooth consistency and an even colour.
3. Portion out the batter between the 12 muffin cases and place in the preheated oven. Bake for about 17 to 20 minutes, or until a toothpick inserted into the middle of a muffin comes out clean.
4. Remove the muffins from the oven and leave them to cool in the tin for 10 minutes, then transfer the muffins to a cooling rack. Enjoy warm or allow to cool completely before storing in the fridge for up to 5 days.

SERVES 1 | VEGAN/VEGETARIAN

10 Toppings for Toast

I love my bread, I love my butter, but most of all, I love a bloody good topper! See which is your favourite of the ideas below, and serve on thick slices of toast for a perfect start to the day.

Smashed Pumpkin & Crunchy Seeds

Roast and mash some pumpkin, season to taste, then top with toasted pumpkin seeds.

Hummus & Toasted Chickpeas

Dry fry a spoonful of chickpeas until lightly toasted, then scatter them over a layer of hummus.

Chilli Smashed Avocado

Mash half an avocado, squeeze over a wedge of lemon and sprinkle with chilli flakes to taste.

Tomato & Avocado Balsamic

Slice a few cherry tomatoes and half an avocado, then drizzle over some balsamic vinegar.

Tomato & Lemon Feta

Slice a few cherry tomatoes, crumble some feta and squeeze over a wedge of lemon.

Garlicky Spinach & Mushroom

Fry 1 teaspoon of minced garlic with some baby spinach and sliced mushrooms until cooked to your liking.

Nutella & Banana

Easy peasy: spread a layer of Nutella over the toast and top with sliced banana.

Banana, Peanut Butter & Honey

Spread a layer of peanut butter over the toast, top with sliced banana and drizzle with honey.

Jam & Camembert

Spread a layer of jam over the toast and top with slices of camembert cheese.

Strawberries & Cream

Spread a layer of cream cheese over the toast, then top with sliced strawberries and a sprinkle of chia seeds.

Halloumi Brekkie Bowl

I was never a huge fan of the standard bowl of cereal for breakfast, so this was my go-to instead. It's a very fulfilling start to the day.

What you need

1 cup (190g) quinoa
500ml water
½ tsp sea salt
½ punnet (100g) mushrooms
½ punnet (125g) cherry tomatoes
½ red onion
1 avocado
1 block (225g) halloumi cheese
1 bunch of asparagus
2 tbsp olive oil
160g kale or baby spinach
2 eggs
1 tsp chilli flakes
Salt and pepper

Here's how

1. Combine the quinoa, water and sea salt in a medium-size saucepan. Bring to the boil over a medium-high heat, then reduce the heat to low, cover the pan with a lid and simmer for 12 to 14 minutes, until the quinoa is tender and has absorbed all the water. Remove from the heat and fluff with a fork. Let it sit, covered, until ready to use.
2. Slice the mushrooms and halve the tomatoes, cut the red onion into thick slices and prepare the avocado. Cut the halloumi into 6 even slices. Trim the ends of the asparagus.
3. In a medium-size frying pan, heat 1 tablespoon of the olive oil over a medium heat and cook the onion and tomatoes for about 3 minutes or until blistered. Transfer them to a small bowl and wipe the pan clean.
4. Cook the mushrooms and asparagus in the frying pan until softened and slightly charred. Transfer to a plate and cover with foil to keep warm. Now add the kale or spinach and cook until slightly wilted, then transfer it to the covered plate.
5. In the same pan (no need to wipe it clean this time), heat the remaining tablespoon of olive oil. Carefully crack the eggs into the pan and cook until the whites are firm.
6. Keeping the pan on a medium heat, fry the halloumi slices for 1 minute on each side.
7. To serve, divide the warm quinoa and greens between bowls. Top with the tomatoes, onion, mushrooms, asparagus, eggs, halloumi, and avocado. Sprinkle with chilli flakes and season with salt and pepper to taste.

SERVES 4 | VEGETARIAN

Big Veggie Brekkie Board

A saviour when brunch with the girls early on a Sunday morning sounded like a perfect idea, prior to copious amounts of wine the night before. My favourite weekend hangover brekkie. Brunching out hungover wasn't so bad if one of these was on the menu!

What you need

½ punnet (100g) mushrooms
2 tomatoes
1 avocado
1 block (225g) halloumi cheese
1 tbsp olive oil
160g baby spinach
2 hash browns
1 tin (400g) baked beans
2 eggs
2 slices of bread
Salt and pepper

Here's how

1. Start by slicing the mushrooms and halving the tomatoes. Prepare the avocado and cut the halloumi into 4 slices lengthways.
2. Heat the olive oil in a large frying pan and begin to fry the mushrooms and tomatoes, placing them cut side down. Now add the spinach and cook until wilted, then transfer everything to a plate and keep warm.
3. Using the same pan, fry the hash browns. If cooking from frozen, fry for about 5 to 8 minutes. While the hash browns are cooking, heat the baked beans in a small saucepan for about 3 minutes until the sauce begins to bubble. Take the beans off the heat and transfer the hash browns to the warm plate.
4. Lay the halloumi slices into the frying pan and crack the eggs into the centre to fry. Alternatively, poach or scramble the eggs according to your preference.
5. Toast and butter the bread, then divide everything between two plates so that each person has an equal amount of mushrooms, tomatoes, spinach, hash browns, beans, halloumi, eggs and avocado. Season with salt and pepper to taste, then enjoy!

SERVES 4 | VEGETARIAN

Courgette & Halloumi Fritters

These are great for breakfast or at any other time of the day! Ideal for a quick, easy and delicious dinner: just add your favourite sides to keep you full.

What you need

½ tin (105g) sweetcorn

1 shallot

1 courgette

1 carrot

1 block (225g) halloumi cheese

2 eggs

4 tbsp wholemeal flour

2 tbsp olive oil

Here's how

1. Drain the sweetcorn, peel and dice the shallot, then grate the courgette, carrot and halloumi. Squeeze out any excess liquid from the mixture using your hands or a clean tea towel, then place the prepared ingredients into a mixing bowl.
2. Crack the eggs into the mixing bowl and add the flour. Stir the mixture until well combined.
3. Heat the oil in a frying pan on a medium heat. Place a tablespoon or so of the fritter mixture in the pan and flatten slightly with a spatula. Cook for 3 to 4 minutes on each side until golden and crispy, then transfer the fritter to a plate lined with kitchen roll.
4. Repeat this process with the remaining mixture, cooking the fritters in batches without overcrowding the pan. Serve them as they are, or with a side salad.

SERVES 4 | VEGETARIAN

Breakfast Pizza

For those mornings when you would open the fridge to make your breakfast, but instead reach for the leftover pizza from the night before. That's exactly where the idea of a big breakfast on a pizza came from!

What you need

1 wholewheat pizza base (see page 176)

½ cup (125g) tomato purée

½ punnet (125g) cherry tomatoes

4 mushrooms

100g baby spinach

1 bunch of asparagus

2 cups (240g) grated mozzarella cheese

3 eggs

1 tbsp olive oil

½ avocado

Fresh or dried chives, to garnish

Here's how

1. Preheat the oven to 220°c. Place the pizza base on a pizza tray or stone and spread the tomato purée over it, leaving a gap around the edge to form the crust.
2. Halve or quarter the cherry tomatoes and slice the mushrooms. Scatter them over the pizza base along with the baby spinach, asparagus and mozzarella. Crack the eggs evenly over the pizza.
3. Drizzle the toppings with olive oil and place the pizza in the preheated oven to cook for about 10 minutes. Keep an eye on the eggs to ensure the yolk stays runny.
4. Remove the pizza from the oven, then top with the sliced avocado and some finely chopped chives before serving.

SERVES 1 | VEGETARIAN

J's Brekkie Wrap

This was another breakfast inspired by a hangover… Probably not the healthiest way to start the day, but it's always nice to treat yourself every now and then.

What you need

1 tbsp olive oil

1-2 hash browns

1 egg

1 tortilla wrap

80g baby spinach

½ cup (60g) grated cheese

BBQ sauce, to taste

Here's how

1. Heat the oil in a frying pan and cook the hash browns for 5 to 8 minutes (if cooking from frozen, less if fresh), turning until golden and crunchy on both sides. Remove from the pan.
2. Fry the egg, ensuring the yolk is left nice and runny. If the wrap has been in the fridge, warm slightly to help avoid it tearing or splitting.
3. Build your wrap, starting with the spinach then the cheese, topped with the hash browns and the fried egg. Drizzle with the BBQ sauce then fold or roll the wrap to enclose all the filling. Serve it like this, or you could lightly toast the wrap in a hot pan for added crunch.

Salads, Soups, Wraps & Bowls

SERVES 2 | VEGETARIAN

Corny Nacho Salad

Nachos are a popular dish found on many menus, generally made with minced beef. Here though, charred corn is the star and instead of the original tomato base I have used a creamy dressing to switch it up. It also requires no baking!

What you need

1 tbsp plant-based butter
2 cloves of garlic
4 large corn cobs
Salt and pepper
¼ cup (60ml) mayonnaise
¼ cup (60ml) soured cream
½ cup (60g) grated parmesan
2 limes
1 bunch of fresh coriander
1 green chilli
2-3 spring onions
½ a red onion
½ a block (100g) feta cheese
1 bag of corn tortilla chips

Here's how

1. First, prepare your ingredients. Cut the corn off the cob, mince the garlic, finely chop the red onion, spring onions and coriander, crumble the feta and slice the chilli.
2. Melt the butter in a large frying pan over a medium heat. Add the minced garlic and stir for 10 seconds, then transfer to a mixing bowl. Put the sweetcorn into the same pan and cook for about 5 minutes or until charred, stirring every now and then. Add salt and pepper to taste, then transfer the corn to the bowl with the garlic.
3. While the corn is still hot, add the mayonnaise, soured cream, parmesan and 3 tablespoons of lime juice. Toss well to combine and let the residual heat 'melt' the dressing so it coats the corn.
4. Add half of the fresh coriander to the bowl with the chilli, spring onions and red onion. Toss again to combine everything.
5. Put the tortilla chips in a serving bowl, add the salad, top with the crumbled feta, then garnish with the remaining coriander and wedges of lime.

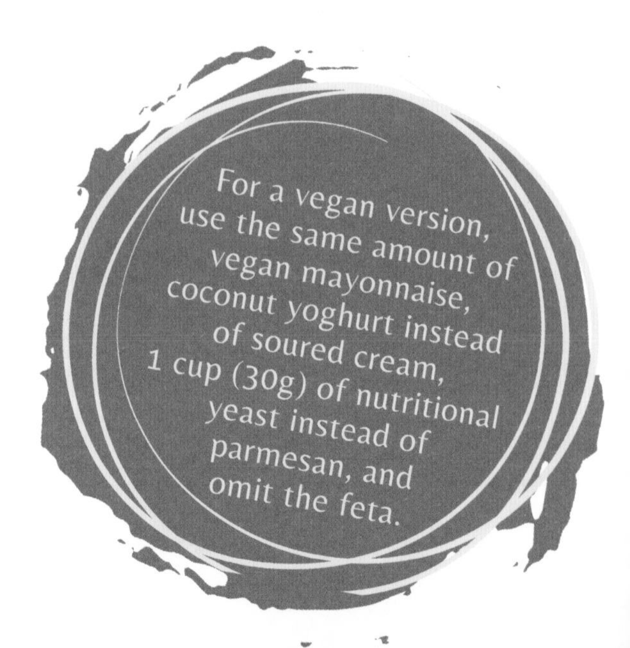

SERVES 2 | VEGETARIAN

Falafel Caesar Salad with Coconut 'Bacon'

For my take on a classic chicken Caesar salad, I've substituted the chicken with baked falafels and the bacon with my DIY coconut bacon bits. This also goes well with my Chickpea Meatballs on page 104.

What you need

1 tin (400g) chickpeas
2 spring onions
2 cloves of garlic
60g fresh coriander
40g fresh mint
1 tsp sea salt
1 tsp ground cumin
½ tsp ground coriander
3 tbsp wholemeal flour (or flour of your choice)
1 tsp baking powder
2 tbsp vegetable oil
4 large free-range eggs
1 cos lettuce
1 packet of croutons
¼ cup (60g) shaved parmesan
Dairy-Free Caesar Dressing (see page 168)
Coconut 'bacon' bits (see page 186)

Here's how

1. Preheat the oven to 180°c. Rinse and drain the chickpeas, then put them into a food processor along with the spring onions, garlic, fresh and ground coriander, mint, salt and cumin. Pulse until the mixture is finely chopped, but not mushy. Add the flour and baking powder and give it a few more pulses to incorporate them.
2. Use a small scoop to portion and form 5cm balls of the chickpea mixture, rolling them between your hands to shape. Place the falafels on a lined baking tray and let them sit for about 10 minutes, then brush them with the oil. Bake in the preheated oven for about 25 minutes, or until crispy on the outsides.
3. While the falafels are baking, boil the eggs in a pan of water over a medium heat for 6 to 8 minutes. At the same time, start assembling the salad. Chop the cos lettuce and add to a large serving bowl along with the croutons and parmesan.
4. Drain and cool the boiled eggs, then peel off the shells and halve the eggs. Add to the salad along with the baked falafels.
5. Drizzle the salad with Caesar dressing and toss everything together until coated. Top with 'bacon' bits and season with salt and pepper to taste just before serving.

SERVES 6 | VEGETARIAN

Mum's Potato Salad

I'm a sucker for anything with potatoes, especially this recipe of Mum's. I used to fight my brother for the leftovers of this; we both love it! It's a crowd pleaser that's ideal for taking to a barbecue or summer get-together.

What you need

1½ kg baby potatoes
3 eggs
1 red onion
2 sticks of celery
2-4 spring onions
½ cup (125ml) soured cream
1 cup (250ml) mayonnaise
Salt and pepper

Here's how

1. Put the potatoes (skins left on) in a large pot and cover with water. Add salt and bring to the boil, then simmer until the potatoes are soft in the centre when tested with a sharp knife. Remove from the heat, drain thoroughly, then pop them in the fridge to cool.
2. Boil the eggs in a pan of water over a medium heat for 6 to 8 minutes. Drain the eggs, leave them to cool, then peel off the shells and mash the eggs with a fork.
3. Dice the red onion, celery and spring onions. Peel and halve or quarter the boiled and cooled potatoes.
4. Gently mix all the prepared ingredients with the soured cream and mayonnaise in a large bowl. Season to taste with salt and pepper.
5. Cover the bowl with cling film and place in the fridge to chill for 30 minutes before serving.

SERVES 12 | VEGETARIAN

Summer Pasta Salad

Another salad you would always find at an Aussie barbecue, and the perfect side to pair with a burger or sandwich.

What you need

450g small pasta shells

1 cup (250ml) mayonnaise

½ cup (125ml) soured cream

¼ cup (50g) coconut sugar

3 tbsp apple cider vinegar

3 tbsp Dijon mustard

1 tsp onion granules or onion powder

1 tsp salt

1 stick of celery

1 bell pepper

1 carrot

2 - 4 spring onions

1 cup (120g) grated cheese

Here's how

1. Cook the pasta according to the instructions on the packet, then drain and rinse in a colander under cold water. Set aside to drain again.
2. In a large bowl, combine the mayonnaise, soured cream, sugar, vinegar, mustard, onion granules and salt.
3. Add the cooled and drained pasta to the bowl and stir well to coat. Finely dice the celery and bell pepper, grate the carrot and slice the spring onions. Stir the vegetables into the pasta and sauce, then toss thoroughly. Add the cheese if using.
4. Serve the salad immediately or refrigerate until needed, in which case toss it again just before serving to make sure the dressing and vegetables are evenly distributed.

SERVES 4-6 | VEGAN

Pea & Smoky Tempeh Soup

This is a great substitute for pea and ham soup. Instead of using ham hocks and bacon bones, I simply marinate tempeh in liquid smoke to create that smoky, meaty flavour.

What you need

500g green split peas
1 tbsp olive oil
1 large onion
2 cloves of garlic
1 large carrot
1 stick of celery
1 large potato
4 cups (1litre) vegetable stock
2-3 cups (500-750ml) water
120g frozen peas
1 tbsp liquid smoke
250g tempeh
2 tbsp coconut yoghurt

Here's how

1. Soak the split peas in fresh water for 5 to 6 hours prior to cooking, then drain and rinse. Meanwhile, peel and dice all the vegetables for the soup.
2. Heat the oil in a large pot, add the onion and garlic and sauté for 2 minutes. Add the carrot, celery and potato and fry for a further 2 to 3 minutes.
3. Pour in the stock and water, then add the green split peas and frozen peas. Use more water to make the soup go further, or if you don't want the soup to be too thick.
4. Add a few drops of liquid smoke, then cover the pot and leave to simmer for about 1 hour. If you like, purée the soup when cooked for a smoother consistency.
5. While the soup is cooking, put the diced tempeh in a frying pan with a drop of oil. Cook over a high heat, stirring often, until it begins to brown. Add the remaining liquid smoke and stir to coat the tempeh.
6. Add the smoky tempeh to the soup just before serving. Swirl a spoonful of coconut yoghurt into each bowl to finish.

SERVES 4 | VEGAN

Creamy Lasagne Soup

This recipe mimics the flavours of that delicious, heavy, baked Italian classic to make a soup you can enjoy any time of the year!

What you need

1 cup (140g) raw cashews
1 tbsp nutritional yeast
½ a lemon, juiced
Salt and pepper
250g lasagne sheets
1 tbsp olive oil
¼ tsp chilli flakes (optional)
¼ tsp dried thyme
½ tsp dried basil
½ tsp dried rosemary
1 tsp dried oregano
½ tsp garlic powder
½ tsp onion powder
5 cups (1.25 litres) vegetable stock
150g baby spinach
Fresh parsley, to garnish

Here's how

1. Put 1 cup of vegetable stock, the cashews, nutritional yeast, lemon juice, salt and pepper into a food processor. Blend until smooth to make the cashew cream.
2. Bring a large pan of salted water to the boil. Break the lasagne sheets into 3 to 4cm pieces and cook for 6 to 8 minutes, or until tender. Drain and rinse in cold water.
3. Put the empty pan back on a medium heat and add the oil with some freshly ground black pepper and the chilli flakes, if using.
4. Heat the spices until fragrant (about 1 minute) and then add the herbs, garlic and onion powders, remaining vegetable stock, cashew cream and cooked pasta to the pan.
5. Bring the soup to a simmer, then turn off the heat and stir in the spinach. Divide between bowls and top with fresh parsley, an extra pinch of chilli flakes or your own favourite garnishes before serving.

Chickpea Gyros

This Mediterranean wrap is usually made with meat cooked on a rotisserie. My veggie version is filled with chickpeas tossed in yummy seasoning and served with crispy fries.

What you need

1 tin (400g) chickpeas
1 cucumber
2 tomatoes
½ a red onion
2 large potatoes
2 tbsp olive oil
Salt and pepper
¼ tsp paprika
¼ tsp garlic powder
½ tsp ground cumin
½ tsp dried oregano
4 pitta breads
Sprigs of fresh dill
½ a block (100g) feta cheese
Dairy-Free Tzatziki (see page 169)

Here's how

1. Preheat the oven to 220°c. Drain and rinse the chickpeas, slice the cucumber, tomatoes and red onion into thin half-moons and cut the potatoes into thin batons.
2. To get nice crispy fries, dry the potato batons with a tea towel before spreading them out on a lined baking tray. Drizzle over the oil, season with salt and pepper, then toss to coat. Place the fries in the preheated oven to cook for 10 to 15 minutes, or until golden.
3. Meanwhile, put a frying pan on a medium-high heat. Add the chickpeas to the pan and season with salt and pepper to taste. Cook for about 8 minutes, stirring frequently.
4. Add the paprika, garlic powder, cumin and oregano with another pinch of salt and pepper to the pan and toss to coat the chickpeas evenly. Continue cooking until crispy but not burnt, then remove from the heat.
5. Fill the pitta breads with the tzatziki, cucumber, tomato, red onion, chickpeas, fresh dill and crumbled feta to finish. Serve with fries on the side.

SERVES 2-4 | VEGETARIAN

Green Shakshuka Wraps

Shakshuka means 'a mixture' and is originally a meat stew that can be enjoyed any time of day. This one is meat-free of course, packed with good green veggies.

What you need

½ a brown onion
1 clove of garlic
1 long green chilli
1 courgette
1 green pepper
1 bunch of kale
1 tbsp olive oil
1 tsp ground cumin
Salt and pepper
3 eggs
1 block (200g) feta cheese
1 tub of hummus (or see page 178)
2-4 wholemeal Lebanese wraps

Here's how

1. Start by peeling and dicing the onion and garlic. Deseed the chilli and finely chop the flesh. Slice the courgette into half moons and dice the green pepper. Remove the tough stalks from the kale, then roughly chop and thoroughly wash the leaves.
2. Heat the olive oil in an ovenproof frying pan. Add the diced onion and cook for 5 minutes, or until softened. Add the garlic and chilli, then cook for 1 to 2 minutes, or until fragrant. Add the cumin and cook for 1 minute, or until fragrant.
3. Add the courgette, green pepper and kale then cook for 6 minutes, or until softened. Season the vegetables with salt and pepper to taste. Make three holes in the mixture and carefully crack the eggs into the spaces.
4. Crumble the feta cheese over the top and transfer the pan to an oven preheated to 170°c. Bake for 7 to 10 minutes, or until the egg whites are set but the yolks are still runny in the middle. Turn the pan halfway through cooking to ensure the eggs cook evenly. Keep checking them and remove from the oven earlier if necessary.
5. Serve the shakshuka with a dollop of hummus and the Lebanese breads on the side.

SERVES 4 | VEGAN

Crispy Tofu Wraps

Instead of using crispy chicken or duck, why not fry up some crispy tofu instead? It tastes just as good, especially alongside the creamy peanut dressing.

What you need

1 block (300g) extra firm tofu
½ cup (65g) cornflour
2 pak choi
2 spring onions
2 tbsp sesame seeds
2 tbsp sesame oil
150g beansprouts
1 packet (100g) crispy fried noodles
4 tortilla wraps
Creamy Peanut Dressing (see page 166)

Here's how

1. Prepare the tofu by removing any excess water with kitchen roll, then dice into cubes. Spread the cornflour out on a plate and roll the cubes of tofu around until coated. Pull apart the pak choi leaf by leaf and slice the spring onions.
2. In a large wok or frying pan, lightly toast the sesame seeds for about 1 minute, then transfer them to a small bowl.
3. Heat half of the sesame oil in the same pan and fry the pak choi, beansprouts and spring onion until the pak choi has wilted. Set aside. Heat the remaining sesame oil in the pan, add the prepared tofu and fry until crispy.
4. Now build your wrap by layering peanut dressing, pak choi, beansprouts, tofu and crispy noodles on the tortillas. Top with spring onions and toasted sesame seeds, then roll or fold up and enjoy.

SERVES 2 | VEGAN

Squash Stir Fry Bowls

Just like loading up a baked potato, you can stuff a squash and eat the whole thing, including the skin. This is what holds most of the nutrients, and as a bonus it's delicious when roasted!

What you need

½ a head of broccoli
3 cloves of garlic
1 butternut squash
2 tbsp olive oil
Salt, to taste
1 cup (190g) quinoa or rice
1 vegetable stock cube
1 cup (140g) cashews
2 tbsp soy sauce
1 lime, juiced
¼ cup (40g) pumpkin seeds
¼ cup (40g) sunflower seeds

Here's how

1. Preheat the oven to 180°c. Cut the broccoli into florets and mince the garlic. Cut the squash in half lengthways and scrape out the seeds and stringy parts.
2. Place the squash halves cut side up on a baking tray. Rub them with a little olive oil and season with salt, then cook in the preheated oven for about 30 minutes or until the flesh is tender. If the squash begins to char on top, loosely cover it with some tin foil.
3. Meanwhile, cook the quinoa or rice according to the instructions on the packet and crumble in the vegetable stock cube.
4. Heat the remaining oil in a frying pan, then fry the cashews and broccoli until slightly charred. Add half the soy sauce and the minced garlic, stirring for a few seconds to coat the cashews and broccoli, then add the cooked quinoa, remaining soy sauce and lime juice.
5. Cook the quinoa mixture while stirring for 2 to 3 minutes, until everything is well combined. Taste, season, and take off the heat.
6. Carve out a section of the roasted squash to create a hollow and fill it with the quinoa stir fry. Mash the scooped out squash and place it on the stir fry.
7. Top your squash bowls with the seeds to serve.

SERVES 4 | VEGAN

Green Pea Penne

Not your standard tomato pasta sauce:
this is made with peas and sure to please!

What you need

500g penne pasta

100g frozen peas

80g fresh basil

1 cup (30g) nutritional yeast

40g fresh parsley

1/3 cup (35g) walnuts

1/3 cup (35g) almonds

3 tbsp olive oil

2-4 spring onions

1 lemon, juiced

Salt and black pepper

Optional toppings

1 tbsp nutritional yeast flakes

1 tbsp chilli flakes

Fresh basil or parsley

Lemon zest

Here's how

1. Boil a large pan of salted water and add the pasta. Cook until al dente, then drain (reserving a mug of the cooking water) and rinse the pasta. Return it to the pan.
2. Pour hot water over the frozen peas, leave for 30 seconds then drain. Tip them into a food processor along with all the remaining ingredients. Blend until smooth and creamy, then add salt and pepper to taste. You may also want to add more lemon juice.
3. Stir the sauce through your cooked pasta in the warm pan, adding a little bit of the cooking water you reserved earlier if the sauce is not evenly coating the pasta.
4. Divide the green pea pasta between bowls and serve. If you like, top the pasta with extra nutritional yeast, chilli flakes, fresh herbs and lemon zest.

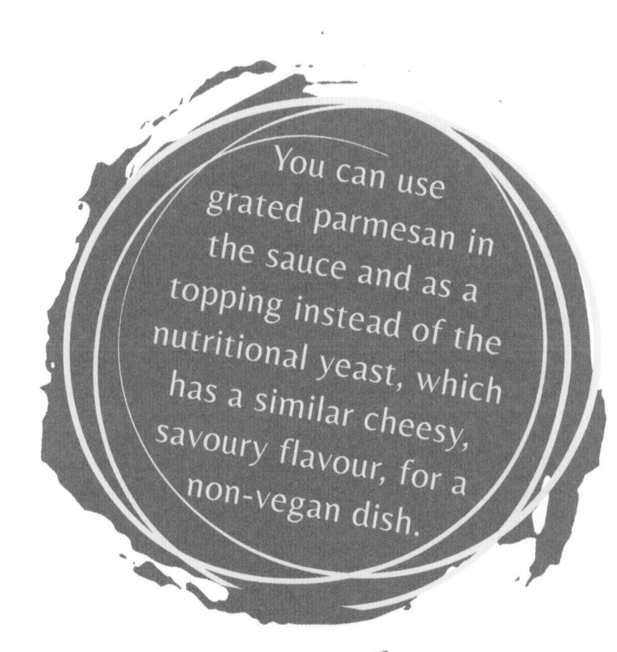

SERVES 2 | VEGAN

Cauliflower Sushi Bowls

These bowls are like a deconstructed sushi roll. I have replaced the fish component with cauliflower florets to make them vegan and just as delicious.

What you need

½ a head of cauliflower
1 cucumber
1 avocado
1 small piece of ginger
2 spring onions
1 cup (250ml) soy sauce
1 tbsp maple syrup
1 cup (130g) cornflour
1 tbsp vegetable stock powder
1 tsp black pepper
1 tsp salt
1 cup (200g) sushi rice
2 tbsp sushi seasoning
100g edamame beans
1 sheet of nori
1 lime
½ cup (30g) crispy onions
2 tbsp sesame seeds (optional)
Wasabi and pickled ginger, to serve (optional)

Here's how

1. Preheat the oven to 180°c. Cut the cauliflower into florets, dice the cucumber and avocado, peel and grate the ginger and slice the spring onions.
2. In a bowl, combine the grated ginger with the tamari and maple syrup. Add the cauliflower florets and leave to marinate for 5 minutes.
3. Combine the cornflour, vegetable stock, black pepper and salt. Spread this mixture out in a tray or shallow bowl and roll the marinated cauliflower in it until lightly coated.
4. Place the prepared cauliflower on a lined baking tray and bake in the preheated oven for about 15 to 20 minutes, until slightly golden.
5. Meanwhile, cook the rice according to the instructions on the packet. Once cooked, stir through half of the sushi seasoning.
6. Pour the leftover cauliflower marinade into a small saucepan with the remaining sushi seasoning and cook on a high heat until the liquid begins to bubble. Transfer into a small dish and use as a dipping sauce.
7. Build your bowl with the sticky rice, baked cauliflower, diced cucumber and avocado, edamame and nori sheets. Squeeze over some lime juice and top with spring onions and crispy onions. Sprinkle the sesame seeds over the cauliflower pieces and serve with the wasabi and a few slices of pickled ginger, if using.

SERVES 2 | VEGAN

Yummy Yellow Turmeric Bowls

Yellow and orange vegetables and fruits are good for reducing inflammation, skin health, boosting immunity and eye health.

What you need

¼ of a butternut squash
½ a pineapple
1 yellow bell pepper
2 large corn cobs
½ punnet (125g) yellow tomatoes
1 tin (400g) chickpeas
1 cup (200g) basmati rice
375ml water
1 tsp ground turmeric
1 vegetable stock cube
1 lemon
Ginger & Turmeric Dressing (see page 171)

Here's how

1. Preheat the oven to 180°c. Dice the butternut squash into small crescents. Peel and dice the pineapple, removing the tough core, then deseed and dice the pepper. Slice the corn kernels off the cob and halve the tomatoes. Drain and rinse the chickpeas.
2. Put the rice and water in a saucepan on a medium heat. Stir in the turmeric and stock cube, then cover with a lid and cook until the rice has absorbed the water and is fluffy when turned with a fork.
3. Line a large tray with baking paper and spread out the prepared butternut, pineapple, pepper, corn and chickpeas on it. Place in the preheated oven to cook for about 15 to 20 minutes. In the last 5 minutes, add the tomatoes so they roast lightly.
4. Build your bowl by arranging the roast vegetables and chickpeas over the rice. Top with the tomatoes, drizzle with the turmeric dressing and finish with a squeeze of lemon juice.

SERVES 2 | VEGAN

Pretty Purple Power Bowls

I love getting creative with colour in the kitchen. Purple vegetables are good for immunity, brain, bone and skin health.

What you need

1 aubergine

1 large beetroot

½ cup (80g) Kalamata olives

½ a red onion

¼ of a red cabbage

1 cup (190g) purple quinoa or wild rice

1 cup (200g) red kidney beans or black beans

1 tsp olive oil

160g red leaf lettuce

Pretty Purple Dressing (see page 171)

Here's how

1. Preheat the oven to 180°c. Dice the aubergine and beetroot, pit the olives and slice the red onion and cabbage.
2. Put the quinoa in a saucepan, cover with water and place over a medium heat. Cook with a lid on the pan until the quinoa has absorbed the water and is fluffy when turned with a fork. If using wild rice, cook according to the instructions on the packet.
3. Place the prepared aubergine, beetroot, onion, cabbage and kidney or black beans on a lined baking tray. Drizzle with the oil and season with salt and pepper, then place in the preheated oven to cook for about 15 minutes, or until slightly charred.
4. When the veg is ready, build your bowl by layering up the quinoa, beans, aubergine, beetroot, onion, cabbage and lettuce. Top your bowl with the olives and drizzle over the dressing to finish.

SERVES 2 | VEGAN

Green Garden Tahini Bowls

Green vegetables and fruits are good for eye, lung, liver and gum health. This salad bowl may look light, but it is in fact fulfilling and flavoursome as well as super healthy!

What you need

1 avocado
1 cucumber
1 bunch of asparagus
50g green beans
50g edamame beans
2 spring onions
1 tsp olive oil
100g garden peas
160g baby spinach
125g alfalfa sprouts
1 lime, halved
Green Tahini Dressing (see page 170)

Here's how

1. Dice the avocado and cucumber, trim the woody ends off the asparagus and green beans and thinly slice the spring onions.
2. Heat a frying pan over a medium heat. Add the oil then lightly sear the asparagus, peas and green beans in the pan. Don't cook them for too long as you still want some crunch.
3. Build your bowl, evenly arranging the baby spinach, seared greens, avocado, cucumber, and edamame.
4. Top with the spring onions and sprouts, then drizzle over the dressing and finish with a squeeze of lime juice.

Mimicking Meat

Mushroom & Lentil Welly

Beef Wellington is an English favourite, usually made with fillet or tenderloin that's wrapped in paté and puff pastry to seal the juices in. When done correctly, mushrooms and lentils are a great replacement for that meaty texture.

What you need

750g brown mushrooms
1 brown onion
4 cloves of garlic
¾ cup (80g) walnuts
1 tin (400g) lentils
2 tbsp olive oil
Salt and pepper
160g baby spinach
¾ cup (90g) grated cheese
2-3 tbsp oats
2 tbsp mustard
Sprig of fresh thyme
1 sheet of puff pastry
2-3 tbsp oat milk
½ tsp ground turmeric

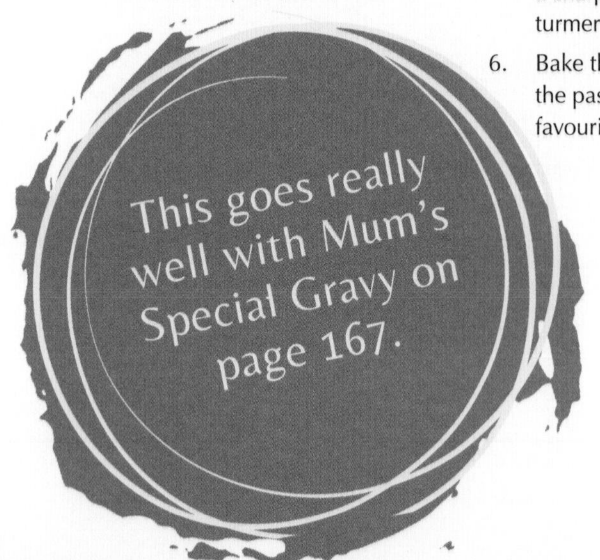

Here's how

1. Preheat the oven to 200°c. Meanwhile, slice the mushrooms, dice the onion, finely chop the garlic and walnuts, and drain the lentils.
2. Heat 1 tablespoon of the oil in a large frying pan. Add the diced onion and sauté for about 3 minutes, then add the mushrooms, lentils and walnuts. Season with salt and pepper, then fry until the mushrooms are golden brown. Transfer the mixture to a plate lined with kitchen roll to absorb the excess oil and liquid.
3. Reheat the pan with the remaining oil and sauté the garlic for a few seconds, then add the baby spinach and cook for 2 to 3 minutes until wilted. Transfer this mixture into a colander to drain.
4. Combine the mushroom and spinach mixtures with the grated cheese, oats, mustard and thyme (discarding the stalks) in a bowl. Stir until everything is well mixed, then lay the puff pastry on a lined baking tray and spoon the filling into the middle of the sheet. Carefully fold the sides over the filling to create a loaf shape. Press the ends of the pastry together and seal, then roll over so that the seams are underneath.
5. Gently cut little slits in the pastry along the top of the wellington using a sharp knife, to let the steam escape. Whisk the oat milk with the turmeric, then brush this all over the pastry to glaze it.
6. Bake the wellington in the preheated oven for about 20 minutes, until the pastry has turned golden brown and puffed up. Serve hot with your favourite accompaniments.

SERVES 4-6 | VEGAN

Tofu 'To-key' Roast

This tofu 'turkey' will have you veggos covered for Christmas!
It's great served as a hot roast or as cold cuts in a salad, sandwich or wrap.

What you need

1 block (300g) extra firm tofu
1 cup (130g) vital wheat gluten
125-190ml water
1 cup (30g) nutritional yeast
2 tbsp cornflour
2 tbsp vegetable oil
1 tbsp chicken stock powder (Massel stock is usually vegan)
2 tsp onion powder
1-2 tsp garlic powder
1 tsp dried rosemary
1 tsp liquid smoke
1 tsp fine salt
½ tsp dried sage
3 tbsp jerk or Italian seasoning

Here's how

1. Preheat the oven to 250°c. Break up the tofu and blend the pieces in a food processor until the tofu has broken down.
2. Add all the remaining ingredients except the jerk or Italian seasoning to the processor and blitz for a couple of minutes, until the mixture forms a dough. If it seems a bit too dry, you can add another few tablespoons of water, just don't add too much more!
3. Once you have a smooth but firm dough, remove it from the blender and knead on a clean surface with your hands for about a minute, then shape the dough into an oval shaped loaf.
4. Lay out a large piece of tin foil (about 3 times bigger than the loaf) and coat one side in non-stick cooking spray, or wipe it down with any oil you have. Sprinkle half of the seasoning you are using in the centre of the foil. Place the loaf on the seasoning and roll it around to fully coat the outside. Sprinkle the remaining seasoning over the top and press it in.
5. Place the loaf back in the centre of the foil and fold up the sides, pinching at the top to seal it up, then twist the ends to fully seal the foil.
6. Place the foil parcel on a baking tray on the middle shelf of the preheated oven. Bake for 30 minutes, then carefully open up the foil and bake for another 30 to 40 minutes.
7. Remove the 'turkey' from the oven and let it rest. This step is important to get the texture right. If you try and serve it before it rests, it will not be nearly as firm.

You can store the 'turkey' roast in an airtight container in the fridge for up to 10 days. It's great for sandwich lunches, broken up in a salad or with roast veggies.

SERVES 4-6 | VEGAN

Hardly Haggis & Mash

Inspired by my travels to Scotland, I decided to put a plant-based spin on this traditional Scottish dish, and it's delish!

What you need

1 brown onion
2 portobello mushrooms
1 large carrot
1 tin (400g) lentils
3 large white potatoes
¼ cup (40g) sunflower seeds
3 tbsp plant-based butter
1 tsp white pepper
1 tsp ground nutmeg
2½ cups (250g) rolled oats
1½ tbsp Vegemite or Marmite
400ml vegetable stock
Pinch of sea salt

Here's how

1. First, prepare your ingredients. Dice the onion and mushrooms, grate the carrot, drain the lentils, peel and quarter the potatoes, and roughly chop the sunflower seeds.
2. Heat a frying pan over a medium heat and add 2 tablespoons of the butter. When it melts, add the onion, mushrooms and grated carrot. Cook for 5 to 6 minutes.
3. Stir in the lentils, white pepper and nutmeg then cook for another 1 or 2 minutes. Now add the oats, Vegemite and stock. Simmer the mixture on a low heat for 15 minutes, stirring regularly. It should become quite thick, but add a splash of water if needed.
4. Meanwhile, preheat the oven to 180°c and line a loaf tin with baking paper. Remove the lentil mixture from the heat, stir through the sunflower seeds and then spoon the mixture into the lined loaf tin.
5. Bake the 'haggis' in the preheated oven for about 30 minutes. To make the outside extra crispy, turn the heat up slightly for the last few minutes.
6. Meanwhile, boil the potatoes for about 10 minutes or until soft, then drain and mash them with the sea salt and remaining tablespoon of plant-based butter to make it creamy.
7. Remove the baked 'haggis' from the oven and leave it to stand for 5 minutes before serving in generous slices with the mashed potato.

SERVES 4 | VEGETARIAN

Chickless Schnitzel

In my early stages of transitioning to a plant-based lifestyle, I really missed crumbed chicken 'snitty' so I decided to create my own version, using tofu as the base instead of chicken.

What you need

1 egg

2 cups (210g) breadcrumbs

1 block (300g) extra firm tofu

1 cup (250ml) vegetable oil

For the seasoned coating

2 cups (300g) plain flour

2 tsp garlic salt

2 tsp paprika

1 tsp ground ginger

½ tsp sea salt

½ tsp black pepper

½ tsp dried thyme

½ tsp dried oregano

Here's how

1. Mix all the ingredients for the seasoned coating together in a shallow bowl. Beat the egg in a separate small bowl and tip the breadcrumbs onto a plate.
2. Slice the tofu into three pieces and gently press out any excess liquid. Dip each tofu slice into the flour, then the beaten egg, then the breadcrumbs.
3. Place the crumbed tofu on a lined baking tray and preheat the oven to 180°c. Heat the vegetable oil in a frying pan over a medium heat.
4. Shallow fry the crumbed tofu in the pan until it's nice and golden on all sides, then transfer it back to the lined tray and bake in the preheated oven for 10 minutes.
5. Remove the baked tofu from the oven and serve with your favourite sides and sauce. I recommend my creamy mushroom sauce on page 167.

SERVES 4 | VEGETARIAN

Beet It 'With The Lot' Burgers

Homemade burgers were a family favourite growing up. The local fish and chip shop also made banging burgers. My "beef burger with the lot, thanks" has become this brilliant beet version.

What you need

400g sweet potato
1 clove of garlic
½ a red onion
1 whole beetroot
1 tin (400g) lentils
Fresh coriander, to taste
60g baby spinach leaves
½ a lemon
1 tbsp olive oil
Salt and pepper
2 eggs
1 tsp Dijon mustard
½ cup (50g) fine breadcrumbs

Here's how

1. Preheat the oven to 200°c. Cut the sweet potato into wedges, leaving the skin on. Crush the garlic and dice the red onion. Grate the beetroot (I suggest popping on some gloves first so your hands aren't stained purple!). Drain and rinse the lentils. Finely chop the coriander and wash the baby spinach. Cut the lemon into wedges and set aside.
2. Place the sweet potato wedges on a lined baking tray, drizzle them with half the olive oil, season with salt and pepper and cook in the oven for about 35 minutes, or until tender.
3. Heat the remaining olive oil in a large frying pan over a medium heat. Add the red onion and fry while stirring for 3 minutes, or until soft. Add the garlic and continue cooking for a further 2 minutes or until fragrant, then remove from heat.
4. Crack the eggs into a mixing bowl and add the mustard. Whisk with a fork then stir through the breadcrumbs, grated beetroot, lentils, coriander, spinach and cooked onion and garlic. Season well with salt and pepper.
5. Shape the beetroot mixture into patties and fry over a medium heat in the same pan you used to cook the onion and garlic. Make sure you flip the patties carefully, so they stay together.
6. Meanwhile, lightly toast some burger buns if you wish. When the patties are ready, build your burgers with any toppings you like. I used lettuce, tomato, pineapple, grated carrot, sliced cheese, a fried egg and BBQ sauce.
7. Serve your burgers with the sweet potato wedges on the side, and lemon wedges for squeezing over the patties and toppings.

SERVES 2-4 | VEGETARIAN

Sweet Potato Pie

Back before my plant-based ways, a potato pie set me up for the day. I lived near a bakery called Blackies Pies that made the best potato pies I've tasted to date! Here's my twist, without the minced beef.

What you need

Sea salt

1 large sweet potato

½ a red onion

1 carrot

2 cloves of garlic

1 tin (400g) lentils

⅓ cup (40g) flaked almonds

1 tbsp olive oil

1 tsp each ground cumin and ginger

½ tsp each ground cinnamon, coriander, allspice and cayenne

¾ tsp black pepper

¼ tsp ground cloves

½ a vegetable stock cube

250ml boiling water

½ cup (90g) dried currants

¼ cup (60ml) oat milk

40g plant-based butter

2 sheets of puff pastry

1 egg, beaten

Here's how

1. Bring a saucepan of water to the boil and add a pinch of salt. Peel and quarter the sweet potato, then cook in the pan of boiling water for 10 to 15 minutes, or until soft.
2. Meanwhile, finely chop the red onion, grate the carrot (unpeeled) and crush the garlic. Drain and rinse the lentils.
3. Put a frying pan on a medium heat. Without using oil, lightly toast the flaked almonds for 2 to 3 minutes until golden. Remove from the pan and set aside.
4. Return the pan to the heat, add the olive oil and cook the onion and carrot until soft. Add the garlic and all the spices, then cook for a further 1 minute or until fragrant. Crumble in the vegetable stock cube, pour over the boiling water, then stir in the lentils, toasted almonds and currants. Simmer the mixture for 2 to 3 minutes or until it has slightly thickened. Season to taste with salt.
5. Preheat the oven to 180°c. Drain the sweet potato, return it to the pan and add the oat milk and butter. Mash until smooth, then season to taste with salt and pepper.
6. Line a pie dish with baking paper and lay one sheet of puff pastry into the dish, pressing gently against the sides to mould the shape. Spoon the lentil mixture into the dish, top with the mashed sweet potato, then place the other sheet of puff pastry on top. Fold in the edges and press lightly around the rim of the dish to form a seal.
7. Brush the beaten egg over the pastry lid. Bake the pie in the preheated oven for about 10 minutes or until the pastry has turned golden and puffed up, then serve hot with your favourite sides.

SERVES 1-2 | VEGETARIAN

BBQ Chickpea Pizza

This is my vegetarian version of a barbecue chicken pizza. A quick and easy dinner, simply replacing the chicken with chickpeas smothered in sauce.

What you need

1 wholewheat pizza base (see page 176)

1 tin (400g) chickpeas

6 tbsp BBQ sauce

3-4 tbsp tomato purée

2 cups (240g) grated mozzarella cheese

½ punnet (125g) cherry tomatoes

½ red onion

2 tsp garlic powder

1 tbsp olive oil

Fresh parsley

Here's how

1. Preheat the oven to 220°c and place the pizza base on a pizza tray or stone. In a small bowl, toss the chickpeas with the BBQ sauce until combined.
2. Spread the tomato purée over the pizza base. Top with the mozzarella, halve the cherry tomatoes and distribute them evenly over the pizza, then thinly slice the red onion and scatter it on top of the tomatoes and cheese. The toppings can go right up to the edge of the base if you like, or you can leave a couple of centimetres bare for a solid crust.
3. Spoon the chickpeas onto the pizza, sprinkle the garlic powder all over and finally drizzle the olive oil on top.
4. Place the pizza in the preheated oven and bake for about 15 minutes until the cheese has melted and the dough is cooked through. Check to ensure it isn't burning after 10 minutes. Remove from the oven and top with chopped fresh parsley to serve.

SERVES 4-6 | VEGAN

Jackfruit Sunday Roast

Roasts were and still are one of my favourite meals to finish off the week. I loved a good lamb roast but nowadays I replace the meat with a nut roast, mushroom wellington or jackfruit. I have mimicked the texture and look of roast lamb here, which really melts in your mouth!

What you need

2 tins (800g) jackfruit
1 brown onion
4 cloves of garlic
500g carrots
500g potatoes
500g pumpkin
3 tbsp olive oil
1 cup (250ml) dry red wine
2 tbsp Worcestershire sauce
1 tsp dried thyme
1 tsp dried rosemary
Salt and pepper, to taste
2 tbsp cornflour
500ml vegetable stock

Here's how

1. Preheat the oven to 200°c. Drain the jackfruit and prepare the vegetables by dicing the onion, crushing the garlic, cutting the carrots lengthways (skin on) and cutting the potatoes and pumpkin into quarters (skin on).
2. Heat 2 tablespoons of the olive oil in a large pot over a medium heat, then add the diced onion. Cook for 5 minutes, then add the garlic and cook for another minute.
3. Now add the jackfruit and cook for 1 more minute. Pour in the red wine, Worcestershire sauce, thyme, rosemary, salt and pepper. Stir and bring to a simmer.
4. Put the cornflour in a bowl and gradually add the stock, whisking until well combined. Pour this mixture into the pot of jackfruit. Leave to simmer for about 5 minutes, stirring occasionally.
5. While the jackfruit is simmering, add the carrots, potatoes and pumpkin to a large bowl with the remaining olive oil and season with salt and pepper, stirring until well coated.
6. Pour the jackfruit mixture into the centre of a large baking tray, place the carrots, potatoes and pumpkin around the outer edges and bake in the preheated oven for about 40 minutes, or until the vegetables are crunchy outside and fork tender inside.

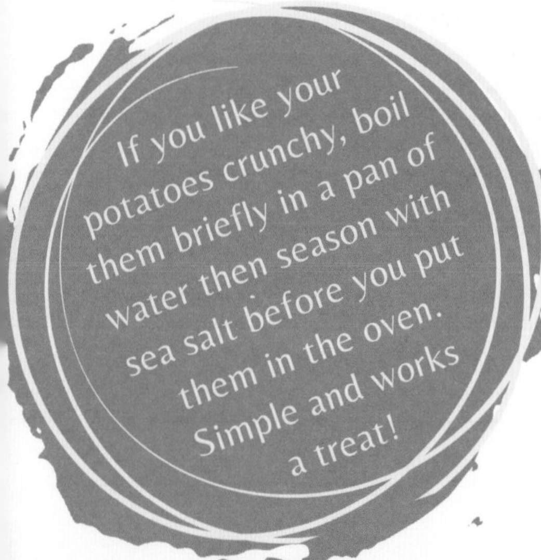

SERVES 2 | VEGAN

Creamy Magic Mushrooms

These are delicious on thick toast, but you could also serve them over pasta, rice or mashed potato for a more filling meal. Portobello mushrooms work just as well as flat mushrooms here.

What you need

1 brown onion
4 cloves of garlic
2 tbsp plant-based butter
150g sun-dried tomatoes
½ cup (125ml) white wine
1 tin (400ml) coconut cream
Salt and pepper
6 large flat mushrooms
160g baby spinach leaves
4 tbsp nutritional yeast
1 tsp cornflour
1 tsp Italian seasoning
1 tsp chilli flakes (optional)
Fresh parsley

Here's how

1. Preheat the oven to 180°c. Dice the onion, mince the garlic and heat a large frying pan over a medium-high heat. Add the butter and sauté the onion until transparent, then add the garlic and cook until fragrant (about 1 minute).
2. Stir in the sun-dried tomatoes with their oil and cook for about 2 minutes to release all of the flavours. Pour in the white wine and reduce the heat to low-medium.
3. Add the coconut cream and bring the sauce to a gentle simmer, stirring occasionally. Season with salt and pepper to taste.
4. While the sauce is simmering away, place the mushrooms on a lined baking tray and bake them in the preheated oven for 5 to 8 minutes.
5. Coming back to the sauce, add the spinach leaves and allow them to wilt (you may need to do this in batches) before stirring in the nutritional yeast which should melt into the sauce. Add the cornflour in the centre of the pan, stirring quickly to thicken the sauce.
6. Transfer the mushrooms from the oven to the pan of sauce, along with any juices. Stir in the seasoning and chilli if using, then garnish with the fresh parsley to serve.

SERVES 4 | VEGAN

Mistaken Steak

On a plant-based diet you can still have your steak and eat it too! When mimicking meat it's all about getting the texture right first. Vital wheat gluten is a key ingredient that makes it happen, and as for the seasoning, leave it up to me.

What you need

1 tin (400g) chickpeas

½ cup (125g) tomato purée

3 tbsp nutritional yeast

2 tbsp soy sauce

1 tbsp Dijon mustard

1 tsp garlic powder

1 tsp onion powder

1 tsp paprika

½ tsp dried oregano

¼ tsp ground cumin

¼ tsp ground coriander

¼ tsp black pepper

¼ tsp liquid smoke

125ml vegetable stock

1 ¾ cups (230g) vital wheat gluten

1 tbsp olive oil

For the marinade

¼ cup (60ml) sweet soy sauce (or soy sauce)

2 tbsp coconut sugar

2 tbsp tomato purée

½ tsp liquid smoke

Here's how

1. Drain the chickpeas and tip them into a food processor. Add the tomato purée, nutritional yeast, soy sauce, mustard, garlic and onion powder, paprika, oregano, cumin, coriander, black pepper, liquid smoke and vegetable stock, then blend until well mixed.
2. Transfer the mixture to a large bowl and add the vital wheat gluten. Stir in with a spoon and then get in there with your hands, mixing it into a dough. Knead the dough for around 2 minutes; you want it to go from sticky and soft to firm and stretchy so that when you pull it, it snaps back into place.
3. As soon as you have a firm stretchy texture, flatten out the dough and cut into 4 roughly equal steaks. Use a potato masher to bash the steaks down a bit, but don't do this too much or they will toughen up.
4. Wrap the steaks individually in tin foil and steam them for 20 minutes. They will expand during this time so don't wrap them really tightly.
5. While the steaks are steaming, prepare your marinade by whisking all the ingredients together in a bowl.
6. Now unwrap the steaks from the foil parcels and place them into a baking dish. Pour the marinade over the steaks, and use a brush to ensure they are covered evenly. Turn them over in the sauce a few times until lathered.
7. Heat the olive oil in a frying pan and lightly sear the steaks on both sides. Brush them with extra marinade each time you flip the steaks over.
8. When cooked to your liking, remove the steaks from the pan and serve with whatever your heart desires!

SERVES 4 | VEGAN

Pulled Jackfruit Burgers

Instead of pulled pork, try this pulled jackfruit. You won't know the difference! Jackfruit offers the same texture and as for the flavour, it's all in the seasoning.

What you need

2 tins (800g) jackfruit
2 tbsp olive oil
2 tsp ground cumin
1 tsp ground coriander
1 tsp paprika
1 tsp dried oregano
½ tsp salt
1 brown onion
1 green chilli
2 cloves of garlic
¾ cup (190g) BBQ sauce
4 burger buns
½ a lettuce
½ a red cabbage
Tzatziki, to serve (see page 169)

Here's how

1. Drain the jackfruit, rinse thoroughly under running water, wrap in a clean cloth and squeeze to dry out. Put the prepared jackfruit in a bowl and shred the pieces with your fingers or two forks. Stir in a tablespoon of the olive oil with all the spices, herbs and salt. When combined, leave the jackfruit to sit for 5 minutes.
2. Dice the onion, chilli and garlic then heat the remaining olive oil in a large frying pan. Cook the onion, chilli and garlic until the garlic is fragrant.
3. Add the seasoned jackfruit to the pan and fry for about 3 minutes, stirring occasionally, until it turns brown and slightly crisp.
4. Now add the BBQ sauce, stir well and then cover the pan. Simmer the mixture for 10 minutes or until the sauce and jackfruit reach your preferred consistency. The longer it simmers, the softer the jackfruit will become.
5. Meanwhile, lightly toast the burger buns under the grill if you wish. Separate the lettuce into leaves and shred the red cabbage.
6. Once the pulled jackfruit is ready, build your burgers in the toasted buns with the lettuce, red cabbage and a dollop of tzatziki in each one.

SERVES 4-6 | VEGAN

Dad's No 'Skippy' Spaghetti Bolognese

If you read the beginning of this book, you already know the story about my dad sneaking kangaroo mince into my spaghetti bolognese as a kid… but don't worry, this is my version of his recipe with mushrooms and lentils instead of poor old Skippy. Again, thanks Dad!

What you need

1 brown onion
1 courgette
1 red bell pepper
2 sticks of celery
2 carrots
2 cloves of garlic
1 punnet (200g) mushrooms
½ punnet (125g) cherry tomatoes
250g brown spaghetti
1 tbsp olive oil
1 tin (400g) lentils
2 tins (800g) chopped tomatoes
2 tbsp tomato purée
1 tsp chilli flakes
1 tsp smoked paprika
1 tsp dried oregano
1 tsp dried chives
1 tsp dried basil
Salt and black pepper
2-4 tbsp nutritional yeast

Here's how

1. Start by boiling a pan of salted water over a medium-high heat. Dice the onion, courgette, pepper, celery and carrots. Crush or chop the garlic. Slice the mushrooms and cherry tomatoes.
2. Cook the spaghetti in the pan of boiling water. Meanwhile, heat a large frying pan over a medium heat, then add the olive oil followed by the diced vegetables. Fry gently until softened, then add the mushrooms, cherry tomatoes and garlic. Fry until the garlic is fragrant.
3. Stir in the lentils, tinned tomatoes, tomato purée and all the spices and herbs. Add salt to taste, then let the bolognese simmer for about 15 minutes.
4. Once the pasta is al dente, drain and tip it into the sauce. Continue to simmer for another 5 to 10 minutes.
5. Serve the spaghetti bolognese topped with black pepper and the nutritional yeast flakes (or grated parmesan for a non-vegan version). Best served with garlic bread!

MAKES 12-14 BALLS | VEGETARIAN

Chickpea Meatballs

Why not try these on a sub with marinara sauce and melted cheese? 6 inch or foot long? Fresh or toasted? You can also freeze the meatballs for up to 3 months, a great batch cooking option.

What you need

1 tin (400g) chickpeas
½ cup (50g) breadcrumbs
20g fresh parsley leaves
2 tbsp nutritional yeast
2 tsp Italian seasoning
1 tsp black pepper
1 tsp garlic powder
¾ tsp smoked paprika
¾ tsp sea salt
2 eggs
1 tbsp olive oil

Here's how

1. Drain and rinse the chickpeas, then combine all the ingredients except the oil in a food processor and blend until the mixture is mostly smooth.
2. Scoop out heaped tablespoons of the mixture, rolling each one into a ball. You should end up with 12 to 14 mini chickpea meatballs.
3. Place on a lined baking tray and brush the balls with olive oil. Bake in a preheated oven at 180°c for about 15 to 20 minutes, or until golden brown.
4. When done, leave to cool and store or serve warm. You could serve these with pasta and sauce, in a sandwich, over a salad, or with sides and a dipping sauce.

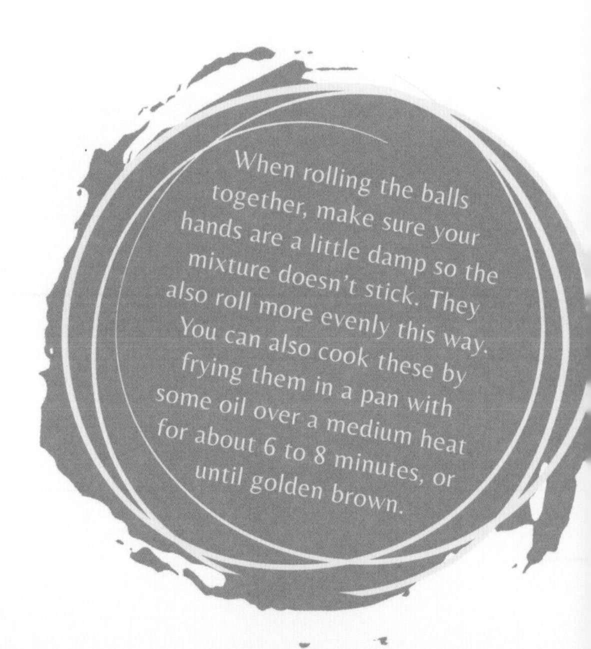

SERVES 4 | VEGETARIAN

Fillet-No-Fish

This was the only McDonald's burger left on the menu when I decided to transition to a pescatarian diet, but in my version there isn't even any fish! Another great veggie burger.

What you need

1 lemon
2 tbsp sweet pickle relish
¾ cup (190ml) mayonnaise
½ tsp onion powder
Salt and pepper
500ml vegetable oil
1 block (300g) extra firm tofu
1 egg
⅓ cup (35g) breadcrumbs
60g water crackers
4 brioche buns
4 Red Leicester cheese slices

Here's how

1. Start by making the sauce. Combine a quarter tablespoon of lemon zest and 1 tablespoon of lemon juice with the relish, mayonnaise and onion powder. Season with salt and pepper to taste, then cover the bowl and place in the fridge for at least an hour.
2. Heat the vegetable oil in a large frying pan over a medium-high heat. Let it get nice and hot while you prep the rest of the ingredients.
3. Drain off any excess water from the tofu and slice it lengthwise down the middle, then cut each piece in half again to get 4 equal slabs.
4. Crack the egg into a bowl big enough to dunk the tofu in and beat with a fork. Combine the breadcrumbs, crackers and a quarter teaspoon of salt, either using your hands to crumble the crackers or whizzing them in a food processor. Tip onto a large plate.
5. Once the oil is hot, dunk the tofu in the egg then the breadcrumb mixture, rolling gently to coat it on all sides.
6. Carefully lay the breaded tofu into the oil, working with only two pieces at a time otherwise the temperature of the oil will drop too much and the tofu will absorb a lot more oil. Fry the tofu for 2 minutes on one side, or until the coating is golden, then flip over and fry for another 2 minutes. Transfer the fried tofu to a wire rack so the excess oil can drain off. Repeat until all the tofu fillets are fried.
7. To build your burger, spread the lemony sauce on the base of the bun, top with a cheese slice, then the tofu fillet. Spread a little more sauce on the upper bun and you're done.

SERVES 4-6 | VEGETARIAN

Taco Lasagne

Who doesn't love Mexican food? Especially with a side of tequila... Take this dish to your next Taco Tuesday with friends, it's always a hit!

What you need

2 tins (800g) black beans
2 tins (420g) sweetcorn
1 red onion
1 red pepper
1 tbsp olive oil
100g tomato purée
1 tin (400g) chopped tomatoes
2 tbsp chilli powder
1 tbsp ground cumin
1 tsp smoked paprika
1 tsp dried oregano
1 tsp black pepper
1 tsp onion powder
1 tsp garlic salt
½ tsp garlic powder
½ tsp red pepper flakes
8 tortillas
1 cup (120g) grated cheese
1 punnet (250g) cherry tomatoes
150g black olives, pitted
Coconut yoghurt, to serve
1 bunch of fresh coriander
1 avocado
160g baby spinach
Béchamel sauce (see page 165)

Here's how

1. Preheat the oven to 180°c. Drain and rinse the black beans and sweetcorn. Slice the onion and pepper.
2. Heat the oil in a frying pan, then sauté the onion and pepper over a low-medium heat. Add the black beans, sweetcorn, tomato purée and tinned tomatoes. Fry for 5 minutes then add all the seasonings. Stir and let the sauce simmer for another 5 to 8 minutes.
3. While the sauce is simmering, start to make the béchamel sauce with the recipe on page 165. Then you can start to build the lasagne in a rectangular baking dish. Begin by covering the base of the dish with tortillas, then add a layer of the bean mixture followed by a layer of grated cheese. Repeat until the dish is full. Save some tortillas for the last layer of the lasagne, then top with the béchamel sauce.
4. Put the lasagne into the preheated oven and bake for about 10 minutes, or until hot throughout. Serve with sliced avocado, chopped cherry tomatoes and olives, a dollop of coconut yoghurt, some fresh coriander and baby spinach on the side.

SERVES 4 | VEGAN

Chickpea Meatballs in Turmeric Sauce

This is a great alternative to meatballs and tomato sauce. I have replaced the beef meatballs with my chickpea ones on page 104. The creamy sauce is really the star here.

What you need

1 onion
4 cloves of garlic
2.5cm fresh root ginger
2 tbsp olive oil
½ tsp ground turmeric
⅛ tsp chilli flakes (optional)
Salt and pepper
250ml full-fat coconut milk
250ml vegetable stock
2 tbsp lime or lemon juice
Chickpea meatballs (see page 104)
40g fresh coriander or parsley
1 cup (200g) rice

Here's how

1. Finely slice the onion and garlic, then peel and grate the ginger - you should have about 2 tablespoons - while the oil heats up in a deep frying pan.
2. Put the onions into the pan and cook over a medium heat for 7 to 8 minutes, or until soft. Meanwhile, cook the rice according to the instructions on the packet.
3. Add the garlic and ginger to the frying pan and cook for another 2 minutes. Stir in the turmeric, chilli flakes if using, and salt and pepper to taste, then cook for 2 to 3 minutes.
4. Pour the coconut milk, vegetable stock and lime or lemon juice into the pan and let the sauce simmer for 5 to 7 minutes.
5. In a separate pan, fry the falafels until lightly browned. Transfer them into the pan of sauce and simmer for about 10 minutes.
6. Stir the chopped coriander or parsley through the sauce, remove the pan from the heat and serve the falafels and sauce over the cooked rice.

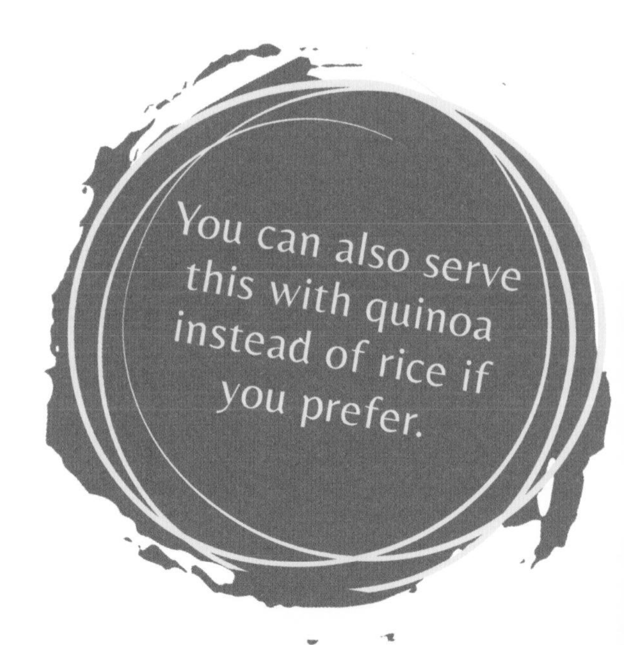

SERVES 2-3 | VEGETARIAN

Meatless Mac

The secret to this burger is certainly the sauce. When I was younger, I used to order a large Big Mac meal with extra sauce on the side just for my fries, that's how much I loved it!

What you need

1 cup (250ml) mayonnaise
¼ cup (50g) sweet pickle relish
1½ tbsp yellow mustard
1 tsp white wine vinegar
½ tsp paprika
¼ tsp garlic powder
¼ tsp onion powder
4 vegetarian patties
4 seeded buns
2 gherkins
1 iceberg lettuce
½ a brown onion
8 Red Leicester cheese slices

Here's how

1. First, make the sauce by mixing the mayonnaise, relish, mustard, vinegar, paprika, garlic and onion powder in a bowl. Set aside.
2. Cook your chosen vegetarian patties as recommended, and while they are cooking, lightly toast the burger buns under the grill. Slice the gherkins, shred the lettuce and finely dice the onion.
3. When the patties are ready, build your burger by layering up the fillings on the base of the bun in this order: cheese, iceberg lettuce, diced onion, gherkins, patties and sauce. Top with another bun half and repeat to make your very own Big Mac.

SERVES 4-6 | VEGAN

Cauliflower & Walnut Mince

This is a super easy and healthy way to mimic minced or ground beef as it captures the same texture. Just like beef mince, it's bland until you add flavour, so season it to your taste.

What you need

750g cauliflower florets
1 cup (110g) walnuts
½ cup (125g) tomato purée
1 tbsp sweet soy sauce
1 tsp smoked paprika
1 tsp sea salt
⅓ tsp black pepper
¼ tsp chilli flakes

Here's how

1. Put all the ingredients into a food processor and pulse until the cauliflower has broken down into smaller pieces.
2. Preheat the oven to 170°c and spread the cauliflower mixture evenly onto a lined baking tray. Bake the mince in the oven for 30 minutes, remove from the oven to stir the mixture then place back into the oven to bake for another 15 minutes.
3. Remove from the oven and serve. Try this with Dad's No Skippy Spaghetti Bolognese instead of the spaghetti (see page 102) or add it to the Taco Lasagne (see page 108).

SERVES 4 | VEGETARIAN

Green Tree Curry

No meat substitute is required in this dish as you have a diverse range of delicious vegetables, herbs and spices that make the curry super tasty. You can add tofu if you like though.

What you need

1 cup (200g) brown rice

2½ cups (750ml) water

1 vegetable stock cube

1 courgette

150g green beans

1 tin (225g) bamboo shoots

100g beansprouts

2 heads of broccoli

1 tbsp coconut oil

1 lime

For the curry sauce

1 red onion

1 green chilli

1 green pepper

1 thumb-sized piece of fresh ginger

2 lemongrass stalks

3 cloves of garlic

Handful each of spinach, fresh coriander and basil

½ tsp each ground coriander and paprika

2 tbsp soy sauce

1 tin (400ml) coconut milk

Here's how

1. In a saucepan over a medium heat, cover the brown rice with the water, crumble in the stock cube, add a pinch of salt and then cook uncovered for 35 to 40 minutes.
2. Meanwhile, roughly chop the onion, chilli, pepper, ginger, lemongrass and garlic (peeling and deseeding where necessary) for the curry sauce. Put the prepared veg and all the remaining ingredients for the sauce into a food processor and blend until smooth.
3. Now slice the courgette, trim the green beans, drain the bamboo shoots and halve the broccoli heads.
4. Heat the coconut oil in a wok or frying pan, then add the courgette, green beans and bamboo shoots. Fry for 5 minutes, then remove them from the pan. Cook the halved broccoli heads in the same pan for 5 minutes, or until slightly soft.
5. Return the other vegetables to the pan and pour over the green sauce. Simmer for 10 to 15 minutes until the curry has thickened to your preferred consistency.
6. Serve your curry over the brown rice with wedges of lime on the side for squeezing over, topped with the beansprouts and an extra scattering of fresh coriander if you like.

SERVES 2-3 | VEGAN

Cauliflower Curry

This warming dish has a gentle heat, so if you like hotter curries use a spicier curry powder or perhaps add some chilli flakes.

What you need

1 brown onion
1 carrot
1 clove of garlic
1 small piece of fresh ginger
1 tin (400g) lentils
1 whole cauliflower
2 tbsp olive oil
1 tsp ground turmeric
Salt and pepper
1-2 tbsp curry powder
½ cup (125g) tomato purée
1 vegetable stock cube
1 tin (400ml) coconut milk
200ml water
1 lime
200g baby spinach
Fresh coriander

Here's how

1. Preheat the oven to 200°c. Dice the onion and carrot, crush the garlic and grate the ginger. Drain and rinse the lentils and break the cauliflower into small florets.
2. In a mixing bowl, combine the oil with the turmeric, salt and pepper, then add the cauliflower florets and toss well to coat them.
3. Tip the seasoned cauliflower onto a lined baking tray and roast in the preheated oven for about 15 to 20 minutes. Remove the cauliflower once tender.
4. In the meantime, heat a saucepan over a medium-high heat and cook the onion with a little oil until slightly softened. Add the carrot and cook until soft. Now stir in the curry powder, garlic, ginger and tomato purée. Crumble over the stock cube, then pour in the coconut milk, water and lentils.
5. Bring the lentil mixture to a simmer and cook for about 10 minutes. Meanwhile, chop the fresh coriander and halve the lime.
6. Add the spinach to the lentil mixture and cook just until it wilts. Remove the pan from the heat, then stir in the baked cauliflower, chopped coriander and a squeeze of lime.

SERVES 6 | VEGAN

Seared Seitan

These are great for taking to barbecues and get-togethers with friends and family, and can be dressed up with any sauce you like.

What you need

2 cups (260g) vital wheat gluten, plus extra for dusting

1 tbsp chicken seasoning

1 tsp onion powder

1 tsp garlic powder

½ tsp salt

1 block (300g) tofu

125ml water

1 tbsp Worcestershire sauce

1 tbsp vegetable bouillon paste

Here's how

1. In a large bowl, whisk the vital wheat gluten with the chicken seasoning, powders and salt until combined.
2. Put the tofu, water, Worcestershire sauce and bouillon paste into a food processor and pulse until combined. Stir this into the dry ingredients until the mixture forms a ball.
3. On a clean flat surface dusted with vital wheat gluten, knead the dough for 1 minute then roll or press into a 1.5cm thick circle. The dough will keep shrinking, so continue to press or roll it back out. If the dough tears, just press it back together.
4. Using a sharp knife, cut out the 'chicken' cutlets. You can decide the shape and size you want them to be.
5. Place a steaming basket in a large saucepan and fill with water to just below the basket. You don't want any water to touch the cutlets. Bring the water to a boil.
6. Spray or brush a light coating of oil onto the basket to prevent the cutlets from sticking, then place the cutlets into the basket. If you need to layer them, spray a light coating of oil over the bottom layer so they don't stick together.
7. Reduce the water to a simmer, cover the pan, and steam the cutlets for 30 minutes. Now remove the cutlets from the pan and refrigerate for at least 1 hour. This will let the seitan develop a better texture.
8. Brush or spray a light coating of vegetable oil on both sides of the chilled cutlets and grill for 3 to 5 minutes on each side, or until they are heated through.

SERVES 4-6 | VEGETARIAN

Southern Fried Seitan

Once you've mastered making the seitan itself with the recipe on the previous page, this is just one example of the delicious flavours and texture you can add to this great alternative to chicken.

What you need

1½ cups (225g) plain flour
1 tsp smoked paprika
1 tsp dried oregano
1 tsp dried sage
1 tsp salt
½ tsp garlic powder
Black pepper, to taste
1 egg
500ml vegetable oil
Seared seitan cutlets (see page 119)

Here's how

1. Preheat the oven to 200°c. In a large mixing bowl, whisk the flour, paprika, herbs, salt, garlic powder and black pepper until completely combined. Crack the egg into a separate bowl and beat with a fork.
2. Heat the oil in a heavy frying pan or deep saucepan. Dredge the cutlets in the seasoned flour, then dip them in the beaten egg, then once again in the flour until fully coated.
3. Once the oil is hot, carefully lay the cutlets into the pan, frying in batches of two. This ensures the temperature of the oil doesn't drop too much.
4. Fry the seitan for approximately 5 minutes per side, or until golden brown and crispy. Place on a plate lined with kitchen roll to drain off the excess oil.
5. When they are all fried, transfer the cutlets to a lightly oiled baking tray and bake in the preheated oven for about 10 minutes per side, or until golden brown and crispy.

128
130
129
131
133
127

Partying with Plants

124

133

132

125

126

SERVES 12 | VEGETARIAN

Cauliflower Party Pies

These party pies are a crowd-pleaser and always first to leave the platter! You can use this recipe to bake a large family-size pie for dinner; just use a pie dish instead of the muffin tin.

What you need

½ a head of cauliflower
½ cup (70g) cashews
1 tbsp nutritional yeast
¼ tsp ground nutmeg
¼ tsp salt
1 tsp olive oil
1 brown onion
2 cloves of garlic
250g baby spinach leaves
½ cup (70g) pine nuts
1 tbsp plant-based butter
2 sheets of puff pastry
1 egg

Here's how

1. Preheat the oven to 180°c and bring a half-filled saucepan of water to the boil over a medium-high heat. Roughly chop the cauliflower and boil for about 8 to 10 minutes, or until softened.
2. Drain the cauliflower and transfer it to a food processor. Add the cashews, nutritional yeast, nutmeg and salt. Blend until smooth.
3. Heat the oil in a frying pan over a medium heat while you dice the onion and garlic. Sauté the onion until soft and fragrant, then stir in the garlic and cook for around 2 minutes. Lastly add the baby spinach, toss until wilted, then remove from the heat.
4. In a large bowl, combine the spinach and cauliflower mixtures with the pine nuts to make the pie filling.
5. Lightly grease a muffin tin with the butter, then line each hole with puff pastry by cutting out circles that are slightly larger in diameter than the holes. Fill the pastry cases to the top with your filling, then top each pie with smaller circles of pastry. Press the lids down gently, sealing them around the edges with a fork.
6. Beat the egg in a small bowl and brush some over the top of each pie. This gives it a nice golden crusty finish when baked.
7. Bake the pies in the preheated oven for about 40 minutes, or until golden and puffy. Leave to rest in the muffin tin for 5 minutes before removing and serving.

SERVES 12 | VEGETARIAN

Pumpkin & Lentil Rolls

Don't be a silly sausage, have pumpkin and lentil instead! These are also great for picnics if left to cool and then stored in an airtight container.

What you need

2 sheets of puff pastry

160g pumpkin

1 tin (400g) lentils

2 eggs

1¼ cups (115g) breadcrumbs

½ cup (50g) rolled oats

2 tbsp soy sauce

1 tbsp tomato sauce

Sesame seeds, to top

Here's how

1. Preheat the oven to 180°c. Dice the pumpkin and place on a lined baking tray and cook in the preheated oven for about 15 minutes, or until soft, then transfer to a large bowl and mash with a fork.
2. Combine the mashed pumpkin with the lentils, 1 egg, breadcrumbs, oats, soy sauce and tomato sauce and stir well. The filling should be sticky but not too wet, and should hold together well.
3. Cut the pastry sheets in half. Place a quarter of the filling on each piece of pastry, lengthways down the middle. Whisk the other egg with 1 tablespoon of water.
4. Shape the filling into a sausage, fold one side of the pastry over the filling, brush the flat side with egg wash, then fold that over the first side to form a roll and seal the filling in.
5. Cut each roll into three pieces and place them seam side down on a baking tray. Cut three slashes in the pastry across the top of each roll, brush them with egg wash and sprinkle sesame seeds on top.
6. Bake the pumpkin and lentil rolls in the preheated oven for 30 to 40 minutes until browned. Serve warm, or leave to cool and store in an airtight container.

SERVES 4 | VEGAN

Mushroom Buffalo Wings

Buffalo wings are usually chicken, and are generally served as a starter or side with some hot dipping sauce. These ones are made with oyster mushrooms which have the same texture when cooked.

What you need

For the mushrooms

250g oyster mushrooms

1½ cups (375ml) vegetable oil

For the batter

1½ cups (225g) plain flour

1 cup (250ml) vegetable stock

¼ cup (65ml) coconut yoghurt

½ tsp pepper

½ tsp salt

For the coating

2 cups (300g) plain flour

1 tsp onion powder

1 tsp garlic powder

½ tsp mustard powder

For the sauce

3 tbsp tomato purée

2 dates, pitted

1 tbsp apple cider vinegar

1 tbsp soy sauce

1 tsp smoked paprika

1 tsp garlic powder

1 tsp chilli powder

250ml water

½ tsp salt

Here's how

1. Roughly cut or tear the oyster mushrooms into your preferred serving size. In a bowl, combine the batter ingredients and mix until smooth. Toss in the oyster mushroom bunches and set aside to marinate.
2. In another bowl, combine the coating ingredients with a pinch of salt and pepper. One by one, transfer the oyster mushroom bunches from the batter into the coating. Place the coated mushrooms on a wire rack.
3. Heat the vegetable oil in a deep pan. There should be 5-10cm of oil in the pan with at least the same amount of space between the surface of the oil and the rim of the pan.
4. One by one, carefully place the battered mushrooms in the hot oil and fry until golden brown and crispy. Do this in batches of 3 to 5 at a time, depending on the size of your pan. Do not overcrowd the oil. Once golden, transfer the mushroom wings back to the wire rack to cool slightly.
5. While the wings are frying, preheat the oven to 180°c. Put all of the sauce ingredients into a food processor and blend until smooth. Put the mushroom wings into a large bowl and pour over the buffalo sauce. Toss to coat, then spread the buffalo wings out on a lined baking tray and place in the preheated oven to cook for 10 minutes. Serve with your choice of dipping sauce.

SERVES 4-5 | VEGETARIAN

Golden Chickpea Nuggets

These golden nuggets mimic the classic chicken versions from McDonald's using chickpeas. Perfect for sharing and dipping at parties.

What you need

1 tin (400g) chickpeas
1 small onion
1 courgette
1 carrot
2 eggs
1-2 cloves of garlic
½ cup (75g) plain flour
½ tbsp Italian seasoning
1 tsp sea salt
¼ tsp paprika
Pinch of black pepper
1 tsp vegetable oil

Here's how

1. Drain and rinse the chickpeas, finely dice the onion, grate the courgette and carrot, then squeeze out any excess water from the grated veg by wrapping them in a tea towel.
2. Place the prepared chickpeas and vegetables into a food processor along with all the remaining ingredients except the oil, adding the garlic and black pepper to taste. Pulse just a few times to combine as you do not want to overwork the mixture, which should still be slightly wet.
3. Heat the oil in a large frying pan over a medium-high heat. Use a tablespoon to scoop out nugget-sized portions of the mixture and place them into the pan. Cook each nugget for 3 to 5 minutes until golden, turning to cook on all sides. Enjoy with your favourite dipping sauce.

SERVES 4 | VEGAN

Tofu Crumble Spring Rolls

Adding tofu to this Chinese takeaway classic makes a more filling snack or meal. You'll need a little patience for the slicing and wrapping, but it's well worth the effort!

What you need

1 onion

200g green beans

2 carrots

¼ of a cabbage

3 cloves of garlic

3 spring onions

2 blocks (600g) extra-firm tofu

2 tbsp sesame oil

½ tsp salt

1 tbsp sweet soy sauce

1½ tbsp soy sauce

15 round spring roll wrappers (made with flour, not rice paper)

1 cup (250ml) vegetable oil

Sweet chilli sauce, to serve

Here's how

1. Start by preparing the filling. Thinly slice the onion and green beans, grate the carrots and shred the cabbage. Mince the garlic and finely chop the spring onions. Press any excess water out of the tofu then crumble both blocks.
2. Heat 1 tablespoon of the sesame oil in a large pan. Sauté the onion and garlic. When they are cooked, add the rest of the prepared vegetables and the salt. Mix well and cook for 8 to 10 minutes over a medium heat until the vegetables are cooked through. Drain off any water that may have seeped out of the vegetables, then set them aside.
3. In the same pan, heat the remaining tablespoon of sesame oil. Combine the crumbled tofu with the soy sauces, then fry the mixture for 10 to 12 minutes. Stir the tofu every 2 minutes until it starts to dry up and turn into a mince. Once lightly browned and cooked through, turn off the heat and combine with the vegetables.
4. Let the tofu and vegetable filling cool for a few minutes while you prepare the wrappers. Separate them carefully and have a small bowl of room temperature water to hand.
5. Place a heaped tablespoon of the cooled filling into the centre of a wrapper, then fold up the ends and roll into a small cylinder, using the water to seal the edges together. Repeat with all the wrappers and filling.
6. Heat the vegetable oil in a deep pan over a medium-high heat. Fry the spring rolls in small batches, without overcrowding the pan, until crispy. Place on paper towels to absorb the excess oil, then serve with the sweet chilli sauce, or any other sauce you like.

SERVES 2-4 | VEGAN

Tofu Skewers

These colourful bites are perfect as a starter, party appetiser or at a get-together with a barbecue. Even better served with homemade tzatziki (see page 169) and flatbreads!

What you need

2 cloves of garlic
1 tbsp fresh oregano leaves
1 tsp fresh thyme leaves
2 tbsp olive oil
1 lemon, juiced
½ tsp cracked pepper
1 block (300g) firm tofu
½ a pineapple
1 red bell pepper
1 yellow bell pepper
1 courgette
1 red onion
1 punnet (250g) cherry tomatoes

Here's how

1. First, make a marinade for your tofu. Mince the garlic and finely chop the oregano and thyme leaves. Combine the garlic and herbs with the olive oil, lemon juice and black pepper. Season to taste with salt.
2. Press out any excess water from the tofu and dice it into cubes. Add these to the marinade and leave for at least 1 hour.
3. In the meantime, cube the pineapple, dice the peppers roughly the same size, thickly slice the courgette, cut the onion into wedges and halve the cherry tomatoes.
4. Once your tofu has marinated, place a griddle pan on a high heat. While your pan is warming up, create your skewers by alternating the vegetables, tofu and pineapple.
5. Place your skewers on the hot griddle pan and cook, turning regularly, until the tofu is lovely and golden on each side. Great served with flatbreads and tzatziki.

Battered Aubergine Platter

When fried without a coating, aubergines can absorb lots of oil, but this batter makes them light and crispy. The brightly coloured Pretty Purple Dressing is sure to get the party started!

What you need

2 cups (210g) breadcrumbs

$^{1}/_{3}$ cup (40g) grated parmesan

20g fresh parsley

1½ cups (225g) plain flour

2 cloves of garlic

4 eggs

3 medium-size aubergines

1½ cups (375ml) vegetable oil

Pretty Purple Dressing (see page 171)

Here's how

1. First, prepare your ingredients. Combine the breadcrumbs, grated parmesan and parsley in a shallow dish. Place the plain flour onto a plate. Crush the garlic and whisk it with the eggs in a separate shallow bowl. Thinly slice the aubergines.
2. Dip the aubergine slices into the plain flour, shaking off the excess. Dip them into the beaten egg, then coat with breadcrumb mixture, pressing firmly. Half fill a large frying pan with oil and place on a high heat.
3. Cook the battered aubergine in batches for 1 to 2 minutes on each side, or until crispy and golden. Remove from the pan, drain on paper towels to absorb the excess oil and cover with tin foil to keep warm.
4. Transfer the battered aubergine slices to a platter and serve alongside the purple dressing.

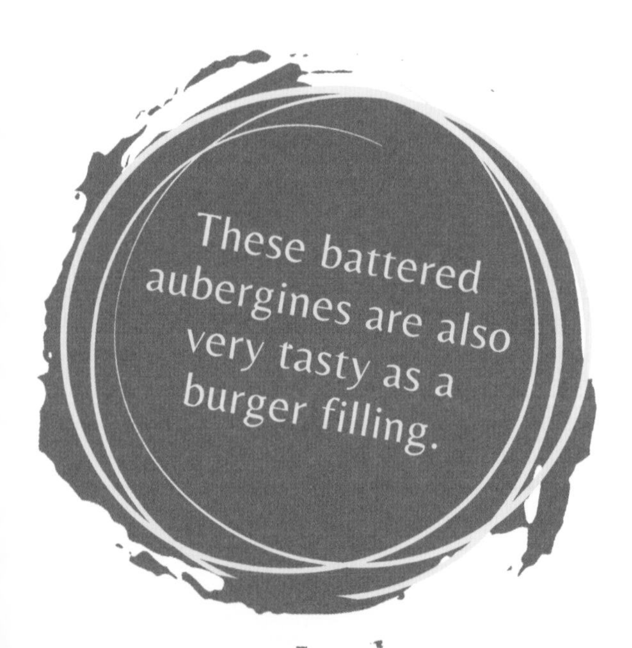

SERVES 4-6 | VEGETARIAN

Potato Cake Bake

Potato bake can be made in so many different ways.
My mum can take the credit for this version, it's a winner!

What you need

6 large potatoes
2 cloves of garlic
1 brown onion
1 cup (250ml) double cream
1 cup (250ml) soured cream
1½ cups (180g) grated cheese
2 tbsp chopped fresh parsley
1 tsp paprika
Salt and pepper, to taste

Here's how

1. Preheat the oven to 180°c. Wash the potatoes and then cut them into thin, even slices. Crush the garlic and thinly slice the onion. Combine the creams and grated cheese.
2. Bring a large pan of water to the boil and cook the potatoes for about 10 to 15 minutes or until softened, but not so soft that they will break apart easily.
3. Drain the boiled potatoes and place them in a large mixing bowl along with the garlic, onion and parsley. Pour over half the creamy mixture and gently mix to combine, but make sure you don't break any of the potato slices apart.
4. Layer the creamy potato mixture into a cake tin, then pour the remaining mixture over the top and bake in the preheated oven for 10 to 15 minutes until slightly golden.
5. Remove from the oven and top with paprika, salt and pepper, then serve hot.

SERVES 6 | VEGETARIAN

Layered Taco Dip

A great dish to take along to a Taco Tuesday get-together. I would always be armed with one of these when invited to dinner.

What you need

1 punnet (250g) cherry tomatoes
100g black olives, pitted
2-3 spring onions
1 tin (400g) black beans
1 tsp chilli powder
1 tsp ground cumin
1 tsp smoked paprika
1 tsp dried oregano
1 tsp black pepper
1 tsp onion powder
1 tsp garlic salt
½ tsp garlic powder
½ tsp red pepper flakes
450g guacamole
2 cups (500ml) soured cream
2 cups (240g) grated cheese

Here's how

1. Dice the cherry tomatoes and slice the black olives and spring onions. Combine the black beans with all the herbs and spices, stirring until smooth. Spread this mixture over the bottom of a 33 by 23cm casserole dish.
2. Top the spiced beans with a layer of guacamole, then a layer of soured cream, then a layer of grated cheese.
3. Scatter the diced tomatoes over the cheese, then top with the sliced olives and spring onions. Cover and refrigerate the dip for at least 1 hour before serving.

Cob Dips

These were inspired by my first job, the good old deli days making platter orders. The spinach dip was a hit and who doesn't love the classic combo of bread and oozy, melted cheese?

SERVES 10 | VEGETARIAN

Spinach Cob Dip

What you need

500g frozen spinach
4 spring onions
1 tin (225g) water chestnuts
1 cup (250ml) mayonnaise
1 cup (250ml) soured cream
1 tsp garlic granules
1 tsp onion powder
1 cob loaf
1 baguette

Here's how

1. Thaw the spinach and squeeze out any excess water. Chop the spring onions and water chestnuts. Mix all the ingredients except the cob and baguette together in a bowl, then leave in the fridge until needed.
2. When you're ready to serve the dip, slice the top off of the cob loaf and scoop out the insides, leaving a 1cm 'wall' inside the crust.
3. Fill the cob loaf with your spinach mixture, cut the baguette into small bite-size pieces for dipping and serve.

SERVES 10 | VEGETARIAN

Cheesy Cob Dip

What you need

4 spring onions
Handful of fresh parsley
½ cup (30g) dried crispy onions
1 cup (250g) cream cheese
1½ cups (180g) grated cheddar
1¼ cups (150g) grated mozzarella
½ tsp garlic powder
¼ tsp onion powder
1 cob loaf
1 baguette

Here's how

1. Preheat the oven to 170°c while you finely chop the fresh spring onions and parsley.
2. Mix all the ingredients except the cob and baguette together in a bowl. Slice the top off the cob and scoop out the insides, leaving a 1cm 'wall' inside the crust.
3. Fill the cob with your cheese mixture, replace the top of the loaf and bake in the preheated oven for 20 to 25 minutes, or until the cheese has melted and the bread is golden on the outside.
4. Cut the baguette into small bite-size pieces for dipping and serve with the cheesy cob.

Something Naughty

MAKES 12 | VEGAN

Chai Doughies

All the deliciously warming spices of a hot cup of chai are mixed into this light and fluffy treat. If you don't have a doughnut pan, try using a muffin tin instead, although they won't have that classic ring shape.

What you need

For the doughies

2 cups (300g) plain flour

½ cup (90g) coconut sugar

2 tsp baking powder

1 tsp ground cinnamon

½ tsp bicarbonate of soda

½ tsp ground ginger

¼ tsp ground cardamom

¼ tsp ground cloves

¼ tsp allspice

¼ tsp salt

1⅓ cups (330ml) oat milk

3 tbsp coconut oil

1 tsp vanilla extract

For the glaze

1 cup (130g) icing sugar

½ tsp ground cinnamon

2 tbsp maple syrup

2-3 tsp oat milk

Handful of pecans, crushed (optional)

Here's how

1. Preheat the oven to 200°c and lightly coat a doughnut pan with cooking spray. Mix all the dry ingredients together in a large bowl.
2. In a separate bowl, whisk the oat milk with the coconut oil and vanilla until well combined. Pour this mixture into the dry ingredients and stir until just combined.
3. Spoon the batter into a piping bag (use a resealable plastic bag with a small hole cut in the corner if you don't have one) and pipe into the doughnut pan, filling each section three quarters of the way to the top.
4. Bake in the preheated oven for 10 to 12 minutes, or until a toothpick comes out clean.
5. To make the glaze, whisk all the ingredients, except the pecans, together in a shallow bowl until smooth. The mixture should be smooth and silky, but not too thin. If your glaze is very thin and runny, simply add a bit more icing sugar.
6. Once the doughies have cooled, dip them in the glaze and, if using, sprinkle the crushed pecans on top. Let the glaze set for about 20 to 30 minutes before serving.

SERVES 10 | VEGAN

Chocolate Cob with Strawberry & Banana Skewers

Chocolate fondue for more than two!
This delicious sweet loaf with an irresistible melted filling is perfect with fresh fruit.

What you need

4 cups (600g) spelt flour, plus extra to dust

2 tsp instant yeast

2 tsp salt

375ml warm water

2 tbsp honey

½ cup (60g) hazelnuts

½ cup (100g) chocolate chips

¼ cup (35g) cacao powder

400g chocolate of your choice

1 punnet (250g) strawberries

2 bananas

Here's how

1. In a mixing bowl, whisk together the spelt flour, yeast and salt until combined. Dust a clean surface with the extra flour ready for the dough.
2. Add the warm water and honey to the flour mixture and stir until a dough starts to form. Fold in half of the hazelnuts, the chocolate chips and the cacao powder. When you can no longer stir it, turn out the dough onto the floured surface and knead into a firm ball. The dough should feel stretchy and elastic.
3. Place the dough into a clean bowl, cover with a clean, dry tea towel and let it rise until doubled in size (about 1 hour 30 minutes). In the meantime, lightly grease a loaf tin.
4. Turn the risen dough back out onto the floured surface and stretch it gently to shape into a loaf or cob, whichever you prefer. Preheat the oven to 200°c.
5. Place the dough in the prepared loaf tin, or on a greased baking tray if you are making a cob. Brush the top with water and use a sharp knife to make 3 diagonal cuts across the top of the loaf.
6. Bake the loaf for about 40 minutes until the top is golden brown and crusty. When tapping the bottom of the baked bread there should be a hollow sound.
7. Let the loaf cool on a wire rack. Once fully cooled, slice off the top and scoop out the insides, leaving a 1cm 'wall' inside the crust.
8. Melt the chocolate of your choice then pour the mixture into the hollowed chocolate cob. Chop the remaining hazelnuts and scatter them over the melted chocolate.
9. Lastly, cut the strawberries and bananas into bite-size pieces and slide them onto skewers for dipping into the chocolate.

SERVES 4-6 | VEGETARIAN

Chocolate Salami

Don't worry, there's no meat in this sweet treat! The name refers to its appearance; when dusted with icing sugar and cut into slices, the chocolate log resembles Italian salami.

What you need

¼ cup (40g) pistachios

¼ cup (30g) flaked almonds

2 tbsp plant-based butter

200g dark chocolate

2 tbsp honey

150g oat biscuits

¼ cup (40g) dried cranberries

Icing sugar, for dusting

Here's how

1. Preheat the oven to 200°c. Spread out the pistachios and flaked almonds on a baking tray and roast them in the oven for 4 to 5 minutes. Keep an eye out so they don't burn.
2. Place the butter and chocolate into a bowl and heat gently until just melted, either over a pan of barely simmering water or in the microwave for short bursts. Stir in the honey.
3. Break the oat biscuits into small pieces, then fold them through the chocolate mixture with the roasted nuts and dried cranberries until everything is evenly distributed.
4. Tip the mixture onto a large piece of baking paper, and using the paper to tightly wrap the mixture, roll it up to form a 30cm long cylinder, pressing gently from the centre outwards to shape the salami and push out any air.
5. Leave the wrapped cylinder for 3 to 4 hours at room temperature until set. If you need to speed up the process, you can put the chocolate salami in the fridge for 1 to 2 hours.
6. Unwrap the chocolate salami and remove the baking paper, then dust the top with icing sugar and cut into slices before serving.

MAKES 8 | VEGETARIAN

Peanut Crispies

Another childhood favourite that stems from my lunchbox. Dad used to pack us a rice bar treat for school most days. Sometimes I make these without the chocolate coating to mix it up, or see the hack below for a Rocky Road version.

What you need

1 cup (280g) peanut butter

5 pitted dates

¼ tsp salt

3 tbsp coconut oil

2 cups (70g) rice puffs

½ cup (80g) dried cranberries

150g chocolate of your choice

Here's how

1. Blend the peanut butter, dates, salt and coconut oil in a food processor until smooth.
2. Put the rice puffs and cranberries into a mixing bowl then pour the peanut mixture over them, stirring until all the dry ingredients are coated.
3. Pour the mixture into a square baking tin, gently pressing into the corners and smoothing out the surface.
4. Heat the chocolate in a saucepan on a low heat until melted. Pour the melted chocolate on top of the peanut mixture and place in the freezer to set. Cut into squares to serve.

MAKES 6-12 | VEGETARIAN

Mint Slice

There are three layers in this mint chocolate creation, consisting of a nutty base and creamy fillings, topped off with dark chocolate. There's no cooking involved so all the ingredients are raw, meaning their nutrients are better preserved.

What you need

For the base

1 cup (100g) almonds

¼ cup (35g) cacao powder

¼ cup (25g) shredded coconut

180g pitted dates

For the fillings and topping

2 cups (280g) cashews*

3 tbsp coconut oil

6 pitted dates

60g fresh mint leaves

¼ tsp spirulina powder

½-1 tsp peppermint oil

3 tbsp cacao powder

100g dark chocolate

Here's how

1. To make the base, blend the almonds, cacao, coconut and dates together in a food processor. Press this mixture evenly into a 23 by 18cm baking tin lined with greaseproof paper and place into the freezer while you make the filling.
2. To make the filling, first blend the cashews, coconut oil, dates, mint leaves, spirulina and peppermint oil in the food processor until smooth. Taste the mixture and add more peppermint oil if needed. Set aside one third of the green mixture (this will be the chocolate layer).
3. Spread the rest of the green mixture onto your base, then return the tin to the freezer so it can set a little.
4. Sift the cacao powder into the remaining third of the green mixture and mix well until you have a chocolate mixture. Spread this on top of the green layer in the tin, then return it to the freezer to set again.
5. Melt the dark chocolate in a saucepan until smooth. Pour the melted chocolate on top of the set filling and place the tin back into the freezer for a final time. Once set, cut the mint slices into your preferred portion sizes and serve.

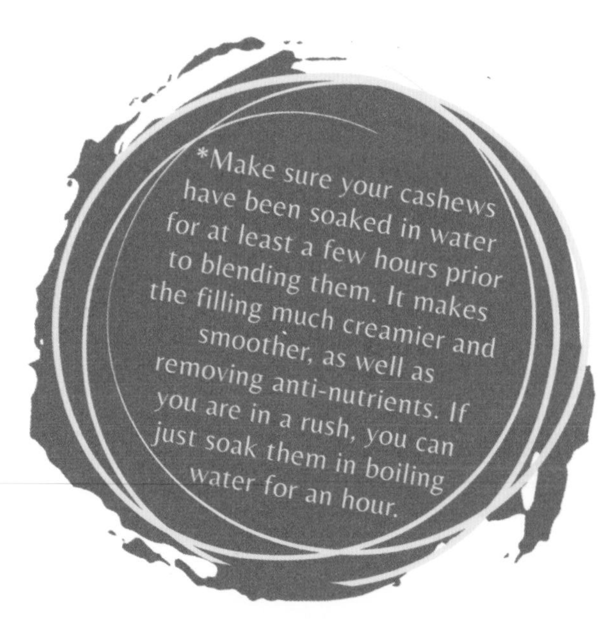

No-Bake Bites

These bite-size treats are quick and easy to make: no oven required!
Choose from nutty or banana and chocolate flavours,
keep them in your fridge or freezer and enjoy at any time.

MAKES 10 | VEGETARIAN

Peanut Butter Coconut Balls

What you need

¾ cup (200g) peanut butter

½ cup (50g) rolled oats

½ cup (60g) vanilla protein powder

½ cup (45g) desiccated coconut, plus extra for coating

2 tbsp honey

Here's how

1. Combine all the ingredients in a large mixing bowl. Mix first with a spatula, then use your hands to knead the dough. Separate the dough into 10 pieces (about 1 tablespoon each) and then roll into balls.
2. If you like, roll the peanut butter balls in some more desiccated coconut. Store them in the fridge or freezer to enjoy whenever you like.

MAKES 10 | VEGETARIAN

Choc Banana Balls

What you need

1 banana

½ cup (60g) chocolate protein powder

¼ cup (70g) peanut or seed butter

2 tbsp water

1 tsp ground cinnamon

1 tsp vanilla extract

100g dark chocolate for coating (optional)

Here's how

1. Combine all the ingredients except the dark chocolate in a large mixing bowl. Mix first with a spatula, then use your hands to knead the dough. Separate the dough into 10 pieces (about 1 tablespoon each) and then roll into balls.
2. Place the balls in the freezer while you prepare the chocolate coating. Place the chocolate into a bowl and heat gently until just melted, either over a pan of barely simmering water or in the microwave for short bursts, stirring frequently.
3. Retrieve the balls from the freezer and dip them, one at a time, into the melted chocolate. Place on a lined baking tray or plate.
4. Put the chocolate coated balls into the fridge or freezer to fully set, then store them in the fridge or freezer to enjoy whenever you like.

MAKES 9 | VEGAN

Flax Flapjacks

Flapjacks are British baked bars which in Australia we would call an Oat Bar or Muesli Bar. This one is still sweet, but by adding flax seeds and using natural sugars it's less of a guilty snack.

What you need

4 tbsp plant-based butter

½ cup (90g) coconut sugar

½ cup (150g) maple syrup

¼ cup (40g) flax seeds

1½ cups (150g) rolled oats

Here's how

1. Preheat the oven to 150°c and line a square baking tin with baking paper.
2. Melt the butter, sugar and syrup in a medium-size saucepan on a gentle heat, stirring occasionally, until the coconut sugar has completely dissolved.
3. Take the pan off the heat, add the flax seeds and oats then stir until well combined.
4. Spoon the mixture into the prepared tin and smooth out the surface.
5. Bake the flapjack for 25 to 30 minutes in the preheated oven.
6. Remove from the oven, cut into slices or squares while still in the tin, then leave the flapjack to cool completely before serving or storing.

MAKES 12 | VEGETARIAN

Caramel Nut Cups

Using unrefined sugars to create the caramel makes this a healthier sweet treat, plus it's packed full of nuts and seeds for plenty of crunch and flavour.

What you need

1 cup (140g) cashews
1 cup (100g) almonds
1 cup (120g) hazelnuts
1 cup (35g) rice puffs
¼ cup (40g) sunflower seeds
¼ cup (40g) pumpkin seeds
¼ cup (40g) sesame seeds
¼ cup (30g) hemp seeds
½ cup (150g) honey
⅓ cup (100g) maple syrup, plus 1 tbsp for caramel
6 tbsp smooth peanut butter
Pinch of salt

Here's how

1. Place all the nuts on a lined baking tray and roast in a preheated oven at 180°c for about 5 minutes, or until lightly toasted. Put them into a large bowl with the rice puffs and seeds.
2. Put the honey, maple syrup (except the extra tablespoon) and pinch of salt in a saucepan over a low-medium heat. Once the mixture begins to bubble, remove from the heat and pour it over the dry ingredients in the bowl. Stir quickly until everything is evenly coated, working fast before the syrup hardens.
3. Divide the mixture between the cups in a muffin tray, pressing down firmly so each one holds its shape.
4. Beat the peanut butter with the remaining tablespoon of maple syrup in a small bowl to create the caramel, then spread this mixture over the top of the nut cups.
5. Place them in the fridge to set for 20 minutes then remove the cups from the tray and serve, or store in an airtight container.

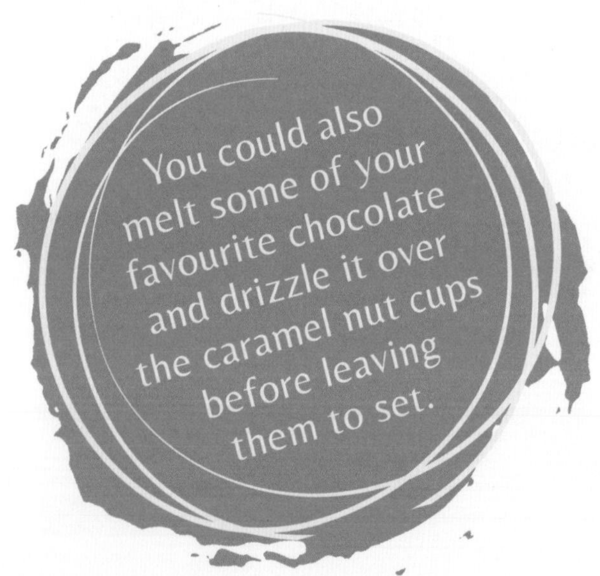

SERVES 4 | VEGAN

Coffee Custard Tarts

You can use any type of flour for this recipe, but I like to use coconut as I find the taste is better and the texture is lighter.

What you need

1 cup (70g) coconut flour

1 tsp salt

1 tbsp olive oil

60ml water

250ml soya milk

2 tbsp cornflour

1 tsp agar agar

¼ cup (75g) maple syrup

¼ cup (25g) ground coffee

½ tsp vanilla extract

½ tsp ground nutmeg

Handful of hazelnuts, to serve

Here's how

1. Preheat the oven to 170°c and grease 4 mini tart tins. To make the pastry, sift the flour and salt into a mixing bowl. Make a well in the centre, pour in the oil and water, then stir until a soft dough forms. Knead lightly and divide into 4 equal portions.
2. On a floured surface, roll out each portion into a thick circle and press the pastry gently into the greased tart tins. Bake for 10 minutes in the preheated oven, or until golden and firm. Remove from the oven and leave to cool on a lined baking tray.
3. Heat the soya milk in a saucepan on a medium heat. Slowly start to pour in the cornflour and agar agar, stirring continually. Heat until the milk starts to steam but do not let it boil. Reduce to a simmer, then add 2 tablespoons of the maple syrup, all the coffee and vanilla, and half the nutmeg. Stir until the custard has thickened.
4. Remove the custard from the heat and pour into the cooled pastry shells. Sprinkle over the remaining nutmeg and drizzle the last of the maple syrup on top of the custard.
5. Bake for 10 to 15 minutes at 160°c. Meanwhile, roast the hazelnuts on a baking tray in the hot oven and then roughly chop them.
6. Serve the tarts warm, topped with the roasted and chopped hazelnuts, or leave the tarts to cool and set in the fridge for about an hour if you prefer them chilled.

MAKES 6-8 | VEGETARIAN

Coconut Rough

This is a lighter way to enjoy a chocolate treat. Simple, but it surely satisfies the taste buds. See the hack below for another version, an Aussie favourite: the chocolate spider.

What you need

250g chocolate of your choice

3 tbsp coconut oil

1½ tsp vanilla extract

4 cups (360g) desiccated coconut

Here's how

1. Line a baking tray with baking paper. Heat the chocolate and coconut oil in a saucepan on a low heat until melted and smooth.
2. Remove the pan from the heat and stir in the vanilla extract. Add the coconut in two batches, mixing well after each addition.
3. Working with 1 to 2 tablespoons of mixture at a time, form rough rounds and place them on the prepared tray. Place the coconut rough in the fridge or freezer to set.

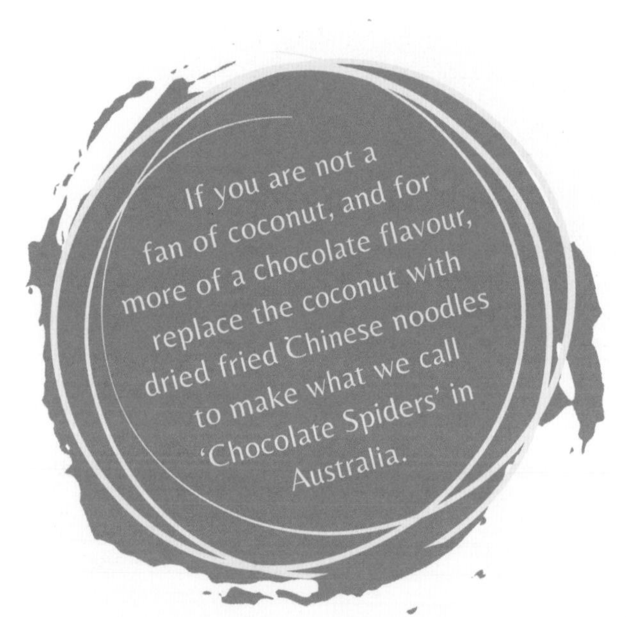

MAKES 6 | VEGETARIAN

Pineapple and Raspberry Icy Poles

If it wasn't the occasional Calippo Frost from the local corner shop after school, it was homemade icy poles or icy cups. This is where the inspiration for this flavour came from - these treats were always a hit!

What you need

2 cups (300g) frozen raspberries

2 cups (300g) fresh or tinned pineapple pieces

1 cup (250ml) pineapple juice

2 tbsp lemon juice

Here's how

1. Blend the pineapple pieces with half of the pineapple juice and half of the lemon juice until you get a smooth purée. Pour this into a jug.
2. Now blend the raspberries with the remaining pineapple juice and lemon juice until you have another purée of a similar consistency.
3. Layer the pineapple and raspberry purée mixtures into a lolly or popsicle mould and freeze overnight.

MAKES 4-6 | VEGETARIAN

Coconut Yoghurt Frozen Fruit Cups

Another favourite childhood dessert Mum and I used to enjoy together. If I wasn't eating Neapolitan ice cream, I was getting stuck into one of these.

What you need

4 cups (640g) frozen fruit

½ cup (130g) coconut yoghurt

3 tbsp honey

2 tbsp vanilla extract

Here's how

1. Combine the frozen fruit of your choice with all the other ingredients in a food processor and blend until the mixture is creamy.
2. Serve the frozen yoghurt immediately in little cups, or transfer it to an airtight container and freeze until ready to serve. It will last for up to a month in the freezer.

SERVES 10 | VEGETARIAN

Fruit Roll Ups

This was my favourite childhood snack; Dad would pack one in my school lunch box every day. Here's a healthier alternative to the store-bought version.

What you need

5 cups (800g) strawberries (or berries of choice)

¼ cup (75g) honey

2 tbsp lemon juice

Here's how

1. Preheat the oven to the lowest possible temperature. Line a large baking tray with baking paper or use a silicone baking mat.
2. Blend your chosen fruit with the honey and lemon juice in a food processor. Pour the fruit purée onto the lined baking tray or mat and spread it out, covering the surface in a thin, even layer.
3. Place the fruit purée in the warm oven to dry out for 5 to 6 hours, rotating the tray halfway through the drying process. Remove from the oven when the purée has set and is no longer sticky.
4. Leave the tray to cool completely, then cut the paper-lined fruit leather into long strips and roll up individually. Store in an airtight container for up to 2 weeks.

SERVES 2-4 | VEGETARIAN

Gooey Matcha Cookie Share Pan

Matcha is a type of green tea that comes in powder form.
It has an unusual flavour and bright colour that makes it fun to use in baking!
Give this a try and you might just discover a new favourite ingredient.

What you need

1½ cup (225g) plain flour
¾ tbsp matcha powder
¼ tsp bicarbonate of soda
4 tbsp plant-based butter
1 egg
½ tbsp vanilla extract
½ cup (90g) coconut sugar
¼ cup (45g) granulated sugar
½ cup (100g) white chocolate chips

Here's how

1. Preheat the oven to 180°c and line a shallow cake tin with baking paper. Sift the flour, matcha and bicarbonate into a large mixing bowl and stir to combine. Melt the butter and place in another bowl. Whisk the egg, vanilla and sugars together until creamy.
2. Mix the dry ingredients into the wet ingredients until the cookie dough is combined, then stir the white chocolate chips into the dough.
3. Transfer the dough to the prepared cake tin and bake in the preheated oven for 10 to 12 minutes. Let it cool for about 5 minutes before transferring the tin to a wire rack to cool completely before serving.

170
167
169
171
167
170

168
166
165
164
171
166
165
Saucy

Creamy Pesto

What you need

½ cup (70g) raw cashews, soaked*

1 clove of garlic

2 tbsp pine nuts

1 tbsp nutritional yeast

2 tbsp olive oil

2 tsp fresh lemon juice

40g fresh basil

40g spinach

3 tbsp water

Salt and pepper

Here's how

1. Put the soaked cashews into a food processor with the garlic, pine nuts and nutritional yeast. Blend for 1 minute to break down the solids first.
2. Add the olive oil and lemon juice, then blend until a smooth mixture is formed.
3. Add the basil and spinach, then blend until a thick paste forms.
4. Gradually add the water to thin out the pesto until it reaches your preferred consistency.
5. Season the pesto with salt and pepper to taste.

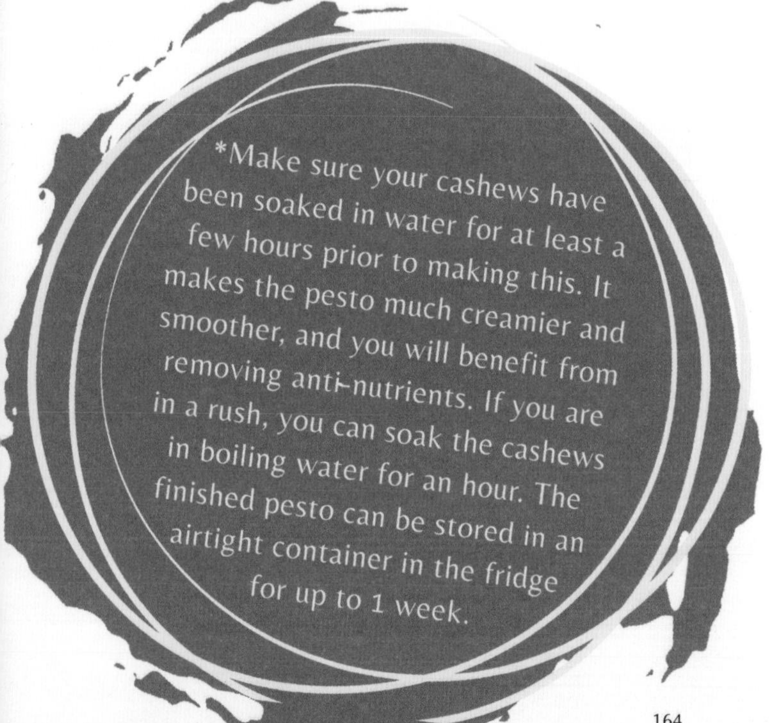

VEGAN

Béchamel Sauce

What you need

2 tbsp olive oil

3 tbsp wholewheat flour

½ tsp salt

¼ tsp black pepper

¼ tsp grated nutmeg

4 cups (1 litre) oat milk

2 tbsp nutritional yeast

2 bay leaves

Here's how

1. Heat the olive oil in a saucepan, then add the flour and mix well until the oil has been absorbed and a paste begins to form.
2. Add the salt, pepper and nutmeg then stir again. Whisk in the oat milk and nutritional yeast, then add the bay leaves.
3. Stir the sauce while you bring it to the boil, then turn the heat down and simmer for about 5 minutes, or until you have a creamy sauce.
4. Remove the pan from the heat, take out and discard the bay leaves, then add the sauce to your meal.

VEGAN

Cheesy Sauce

What you need

1 tin (400g) cannellini beans

½ cup (125ml) soya milk

6-8 tbsp nutritional yeast

3 tbsp fresh lemon juice

1 tsp salt

¼ tsp black pepper

Here's how

1. Drain and rinse the cannellini beans, then put them into a food processor.
2. Add all the remaining ingredients to the processor and blend until smooth.
3. Store leftovers in the fridge for up to 4 days.

VEGAN

Chilli Sauce

What you need

250g fresh chillies

4 cloves of garlic

1 tbsp salt

¼ cup (45g) brown sugar

½ cup (125ml) white vinegar

Here's how

1. Put the chillies, garlic, salt and sugar in a food processor and pulse until chopped.
2. Transfer the mixture to a saucepan and stir in the vinegar. Bring to the boil, then reduce the heat and simmer for 15 minutes until thickened.
3. To test whether the sauce is ready, scrape the base of the pan with a spatula. If the sauce separates and the spatula leaves a trail, it's ready.
4. Strain the chilli sauce through a fine sieve and store in a glass jar until serving.

VEGAN

Creamy Peanut Dressing

What you need

½ cup (140g) peanut butter

2 cloves of garlic, minced

½ tbsp grated fresh ginger

2 tbsp soy sauce

2 tbsp lime juice

½ tbsp maple syrup

¼-½ tsp red pepper flakes (optional)

2-4 tbsp filtered water

Here's how

1. Put all the ingredients except the water into a bowl and mix until well combined.
2. Add 2 tablespoons of the filtered water and stir gently until incorporated, then continue adding water 1 teaspoon at a time until the dressing reaches your preferred consistency.
3. Leave to stand for 5 minutes to allow flavours to combine before serving.
4. Refrigerate leftovers in a sealed container for up to 10 days.

VEGAN

Mum's Special Gravy

What you need

2 cups (500ml) water

4 tbsp plain flour

1 tbsp plant-based butter

1 beef stock cube

1 chicken stock cube

½ tsp onion powder

Salt and pepper

Here's how

1. Put all the ingredients into a saucepan and bring to the boil. Stir continuously until well combined, then simmer the gravy for about 10 minutes, before serving with your meal.
2. For beef and chicken stock cubes, I always use the Massel brand as they are vegan. To make an OMG (onion and mushroom gravy) just add sliced and sautéed onion and mushrooms.

VEGAN

Creamy Mushroom Sauce

What you need

300g button mushrooms

2 cloves of garlic

1 brown onion

1 tbsp olive oil

1 tbsp nut butter

¼ tsp grated nutmeg

Salt and pepper, to taste

1½ cups (375ml) oat milk

1 tbsp nutritional yeast

1 tbsp cornflour

Here's how

1. Slice the mushrooms, mince the garlic and dice the onion. Heat the oil in a frying pan and cook the garlic, onion and nut butter over a medium heat until fragrant and browned.
2. Add the mushrooms to the pan and stir well. Cook until the mushrooms have softened, then add the nutmeg and cook for a further 2 to 3 minutes. Season with salt and pepper.
3. Pour in the oat milk, then quickly stir in the nutritional yeast and cornflour. Mix well and then leave the sauce to simmer for 5 minutes before serving with your meal.

Dairy-Free Caesar Dressing

What you need

½ cup (70g) raw cashews, soaked*
½ cup (125ml) water
3 tbsp lemon juice
1 tbsp Dijon mustard
½ tbsp Worcestershire sauce
2 tsp nutritional yeast
2 tsp capers
1 clove of garlic
½ tsp sea salt, or to taste
⅛ tsp black pepper, or to taste

Here's how

1. Place all the ingredients except the salt and pepper in a food processor.
2. Blend until smooth then season with the salt and pepper to taste.
3. Add more water if necessary to reach a dressing-like consistency.

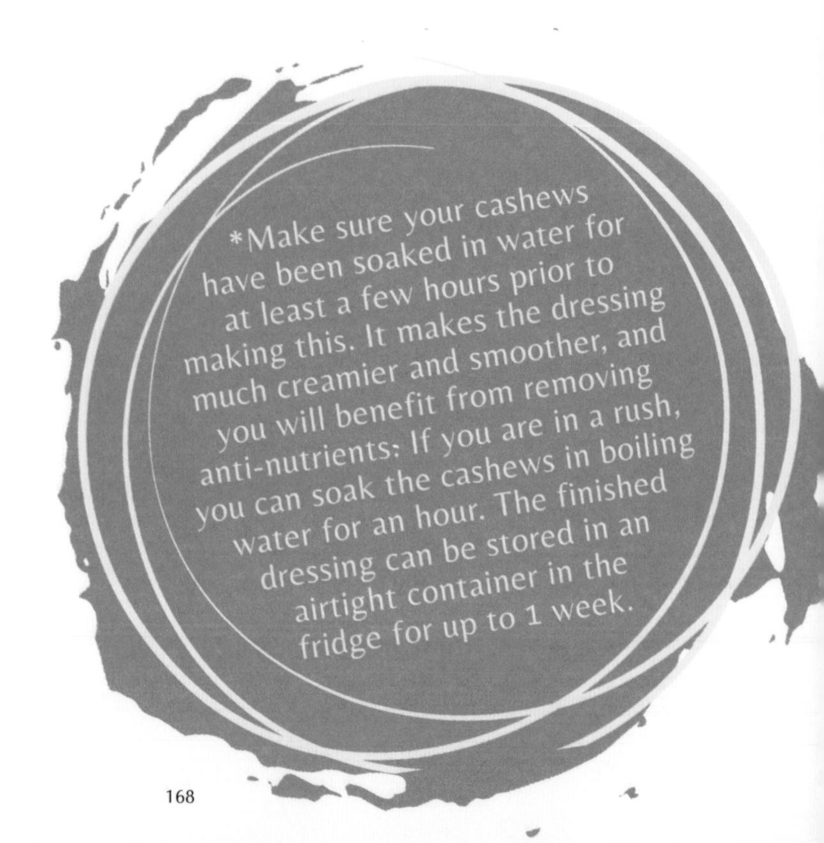

Dairy-Free Tzatziki

What you need

1 large cucumber
Pinch of salt
3 tbsp chopped fresh dill
1 tsp chopped fresh mint
2 cloves of garlic
1 cup (250ml) coconut yoghurt
1 tbsp lemon juice
1 tbsp olive oil

Here's how

1. Grate the cucumber into a colander and squeeze out the excess water. Sprinkle the grated cucumber with salt and leave for 5 minutes for more moisture to drip out.
2. Meanwhile, chop the fresh herbs and mince the garlic. Combine the yoghurt, lemon juice and olive oil in a bowl, then add all the prepared ingredients and mix well until creamy.

VEGAN

Creamy Avocado Dressing

What you need

1 avocado

1 lime, juiced

1 tbsp maple syrup

20g fresh basil leaves

¼ cup (60ml) apple cider vinegar

¼ cup (60ml) water

¼ tsp garlic powder

Salt and pepper, to taste

Here's how

1. Halve and destone the avocado, scoop out the flesh and put this into a food processor.
2. Add all the remaining ingredients and blend until smooth and creamy.
3. Add a little more water if you prefer a thinner consistency.
4. Store leftovers in the fridge for up to 1 week.

VEGAN

Green Tahini Dressing

What you need

20g fresh coriander

20g fresh parsley

¼ cup (60ml) water

3 tbsp olive oil

2 tbsp tahini

1 lime, juiced

1 clove of garlic

⅛ tsp salt

Here's how

1. Put all the ingredients into a food processor and blend for about 20 seconds, or until well combined.
2. Store leftovers in the fridge for up to 4 days.

VEGAN

Ginger & Turmeric Dressing

What you need

3 tbsp olive oil
½ cup (125ml) water
½ a lemon, zested
3 tbsp fresh lemon juice
1 tbsp ginger purée
1 clove of garlic
2 tsp honey
1 tsp ground turmeric
½ tsp fine sea salt
Black pepper, to taste

Here's how

1. Put all the ingredients into a food processor and blend until smooth. Taste and add more salt and lemon juice as desired.
2. Store leftovers in the fridge for up to 1 week.

VEGAN

Pretty Purple Dressing

What you need

½ cup (70g) cashews, soaked*
100g blueberries
20g fresh parsley
¼ cup (60ml) water
1 clove of garlic
2 tbsp lemon juice
2 tbsp nutritional yeast
1 tbsp olive oil
1 tsp balsamic vinegar
Salt and pepper, to taste

Here's how

1. *Make sure your cashews have been soaked in water for at least a few hours prior to making this. It makes the dressing much creamier and smoother, and you will benefit from removing anti-nutrients. If you are in a rush, you can soak the cashews in boiling water for an hour.
2. Put all the ingredients except the water into a food processor and blend until smooth.
3. Add the water in stages until the dressing reaches your preferred consistency.
4. The finished dressing can be stored in an airtight container in the fridge for up to 1 week.

Make it
from Scratch
ELITE

MAKES 10-12 SLICES | VEGETARIAN

Seeded Spelt Bread

Making your own bread can be very therapeutic and requires very little hands-on time, just a bit of waiting while it proves and bakes. Spelt is an ancient grain with lots of flavour and nutrients.

What you need

4 cups (600g) spelt flour, plus extra for dusting

2 tbsp sunflower seeds

2 tbsp flax seeds

2 tbsp sesame seeds

2 tbsp pumpkin seeds

2 tsp instant yeast

2 tsp salt

1½ cups (375ml) warm water

2 tbsp honey

Here's how

1. Set half of the flax, sesame, sunflower and pumpkin seeds aside. Put the flour, remaining seeds, yeast and salt in a mixing bowl and mix everything together. Dust a clean surface with the extra spelt flour.
2. Add the warm water and honey to the dry ingredients and stir until a dough starts to form. When you can no longer stir, transfer the dough onto the floured surface and knead into a firm ball. The dough should be stretchy and elastic.
3. Place the ball of dough into a clean bowl, cover with a tea towel and let it rise until doubled in size (about 1 hour 30 minutes). In the meantime, lightly grease a loaf tin.
4. Turn out the risen dough on a floured surface and stretch it out gently. Shape the dough into a loaf or cob, whichever you prefer. Preheat the oven to 200°c.
5. Place the dough in the prepared loaf tin, or on a lightly greased, sturdy baking tray for a cob. Brush the top with water and sprinkle with the remaining seeds. With a sharp knife, make three diagonal cuts across the top of the dough.
6. Bake the bread for about 40 minutes until the top is golden brown and crusty. When you tap the bottom of the baked loaf or cob, it should sound hollow.
7. Transfer to a wire rack and wait until the bread has completely cooled before slicing.

MAKES 1 PIZZA BASE | VEGAN

Dough It Yourself

This is a super easy recipe for pizza bases; simply mix all the ingredients together in a bowl, knead and wait. Then add your toppings to make and bake!

What you need

1 cup (250ml) lukewarm water
2 tsp active dry yeast
1 tsp coconut sugar
2 tbsp olive oil
½ tsp sea salt
2½ cups (375g) wholewheat flour

Here's how

1. Mix the water with the yeast and sugar in a large bowl. Let it stand for 3 to 4 minutes until the yeast begins to foam.
2. Add the olive oil and salt to the bowl, then stir in most of the flour (reserving about ½ cup/60g) until the dough starts to come together.
3. If the dough is still too wet, add the remaining flour a bit at a time and knead. The dough should pull itself into a ball as you stir, but should still be slightly sticky to the touch. If the dough is too dry, add a splash of water or olive oil and knead to work the liquid in.
4. Cover the dough with a tea towel and let it rest for at least 10 minutes at room temperature. If you have more time, let it rest for up to an hour to develop more flavour.
5. Turn out the rested dough on a lightly floured surface, then roll and shape into a pizza base.
6. Top with your favourite sauce, cheese and toppings then bake according to your favourite method. Try making my BBQ Chickpea Pizza (see page 92) or Breakfast Pizza (see page 44).

SERVES 4 | VEGETARIAN

On The Go Granola

This is ideal to make ahead of a new week, for those rushed mornings when you're really hungry but want something healthy to start the day.

What you need

2 tbsp coconut oil

2 cups (200g) rolled oats

1 cup (100g) almonds

½ cup (80g) pumpkin seeds

1 tsp vanilla extract

4 tbsp honey

Here's how

1. Preheat the oven to 180°c and melt the coconut oil in a pan over a gentle heat.
2. Combine the melted coconut oil with all the other ingredients in a large mixing bowl until the oats, almonds and seeds are well coated.
3. Spread the granola out on a lined baking tray and bake in the preheated oven for 8 to 10 minutes. Remove from the oven and allow to cool before eating.

SERVES 2-4 | VEGAN/VEGETARIAN

Three Kinds of Hummus

Hummus is so versatile: you can have it with crackers and veggie sticks, lathered into sandwiches and wraps, as a topping for salad bowls or even on toast!

What you need

Chickpea Hummus

1 tin (400g) chickpeas

3 tbsp olive oil, plus extra to serve

3 tbsp lemon juice

3 tbsp tahini

1 clove of garlic

1 tsp sea salt

¼ tsp ground cumin

Carrot Hummus

1 tin (400g) chickpeas

2 carrots, peeled and grated

2 tsp honey

3 tbsp olive oil, plus extra to serve

3 tbsp lemon juice

3 tbsp tahini

1 clove of garlic

1 tsp sea salt

¼ tsp ground cumin

Green Pea Hummus

1 tin (400g) chickpeas

300g frozen green peas, lightly cooked or rinsed well under hot water

40g fresh mint leaves

3 tbsp olive oil, plus extra to serve

3 tbsp lemon juice

3 tbsp tahini

1 clove of garlic

1 tsp sea salt

Here's how

1. Drain and rinse the chickpeas, then put them into a food processor.
2. Add all the remaining ingredients for your chosen hummus to the processor.
3. Blend until the mixture has a smooth consistency.
4. Taste to check the seasoning. Add more salt if needed.
5. Top the hummus with a drizzle of olive oil to serve.

SERVES 2-4 | VEGAN

Dukkah

This is a Middle Eastern dip which goes really well with bread and oils for a snack. It's also great as part of a cheeseboard or meze-style spread.

What you need

1 cup (120g) dry roasted peanuts

½ cup (75g) sesame seeds

2 tbsp coriander seeds

2 tbsp cumin seeds

1½ tsp black pepper

1 tsp salt

Here's how

1. Heat a frying pan over a medium heat with no oil. Toast the sesame seeds in the hot dry pan, stirring continuously, until golden. This should take 2 to 3 minutes. Set aside.
2. Now toast the coriander and cumin seeds in the same pan, stirring frequently for 1 to 2 minutes until they pop. Do not overcook.
3. Tip the coriander and cumin seeds into a food processor and pulse until finely chopped, then transfer them to a bowl. Put half of the toasted sesame seeds into the food processor with the peanuts and pulse until chopped. Add them to the spices.
4. Combine the chopped peanut, sesame and spice mixture with the remaining toasted sesame seeds, pepper and salt. Mix well, then serve alongside oils and crusty bread.

SERVES 2-4| VEGAN

Seeded Crackers

This is a fun and easy way to make your own savoury snacks. These crackers are packed with crunch and super versatile; serve them with cheeseboards, dips, soups and more.

What you need

1½ cups (375ml) water

¾ cup (120g) sunflower seeds

¾ cup (120g) pumpkin seeds

½ cup (75g) sesame seeds

½ cup (100g) chia seeds

¼ cup (40g) flax seeds

1 tbsp dried herbs of your choice (I used thyme)

1 tsp salt

Here's how

1. Preheat the oven to 170°c. Combine all the ingredients in a mixing bowl and leave for 10 to 15 minutes for the seeds to soak up the water.
2. Stir well, then split the mixture between two lined baking trays and spread thinly. The ideal thickness is about 3 or 4mm. Too thin and the crackers will be very fragile, too thick and they'll be more like a seed cookie than a cracker.
3. Bake the sheets for 1 hour (switching the trays around halfway through) or until golden brown and crisp. If the crackers don't feel crisp after an hour, return the trays to the oven for another 5 to 10 minutes.
4. Remove from the oven, leave to cool, then break or cut the crackers into the shapes you like. Store in an airtight container.

MAKES 12-14 | VEGAN

No Faff Falafels

Falafels are generally deep-fried, but you can bake these ones in the oven without compromising the crunch. Very versatile and great in salads, pittas or wraps.

What you need

1 tin (400g) chickpeas

½ a large onion

40g fresh parsley

20g fresh coriander

4 cloves of garlic

2 tsp ground cumin

1 tsp ground coriander

1 tsp sea salt

1 tsp baking powder

4 tbsp wholemeal flour (or flour of your choice)

1 tbsp olive oil

Here's how

1. Preheat the oven to 180°c. Drain and rinse the chickpeas, roughly chop the onion then put them both into a food processor along with the herbs, peeled garlic, spices and salt.
2. Pulse until the mixture is chopped but not puréed, then transfer it to a bowl and add the baking powder and flour, stirring until well combined.
3. Form the falafel mixture into little balls about the size of one heaped tablespoon each. Place on a lined baking tray.
4. Brush the falafels with olive oil and bake in the preheated oven for about 20 to 25 minutes, or until golden. Turn each falafel after 10 to 12 minutes to ensure they cook evenly. When done, leave to cool and store or serve warm.

The first of these two recipes creates 'bacon bits' that are great for scattering over salads and soups. The second is for strips that more closely resemble a bacon rasher. Both have the same salty, savoury hit of flavour without the meat!

SERVES 2-4 | VEGAN

Bacon, You Reckon?

What you need

2 tbsp liquid smoke
1 tbsp soy sauce
1 tbsp maple syrup
1 tbsp water
250g coconut chips
1 tsp smoked paprika

Here's how

1. Preheat the oven to 160°c and combine all the liquid ingredients in a bowl. Add the coconut chips and gently toss until evenly coated.
2. Sprinkle over most of the paprika, then toss until evenly mixed in. Spread the coconut chips on a tray lined with baking paper and lightly sprinkle more paprika on top.
3. Bake for 20 to 25 minutes in the oven, flipping the coconut chips every 5 minutes to ensure they cook evenly. Keep a close eye on these as they can burn easily.

SERVES 2-4 | VEGAN

Barely Bacon Strips

What you need

6 sheets of rice paper
3 tbsp soy sauce
2 tbsp vegetable oil
2 tbsp nutritional yeast
1 tsp maple syrup
1 tsp liquid smoke
½ tsp smoked paprika
½ tsp garlic powder
Pinch of black pepper

Here's how

1. Preheat the oven to 180°c and combine all the ingredients except the rice paper in a large mixing bowl. Stir until well mixed and then set aside. Fill another bowl with water.
2. Line a large tray with baking paper and cut the rice paper carefully into big strips of equal size. You should use a very sharp knife or kitchen scissors to do this.
3. Now lay two of the strips on top of each other and pull through the bowl of water to make them stick together. Pull the double-layered strip through the marinade, let it drain a little bit and then lay it on the prepared baking tray. Repeat until all the strips are used up.
4. Bake the marinated rice paper 'bacon' in the preheated oven for about 7 to 8 minutes until it is partially crunchy but still a bit soft.

Tofu & Tempeh Marinades

These recipes each make enough marinade for 1 block of tofu or tempeh. Choose from barbecue, chilli, honey soy and Mexican flavours to spice up any meal.

What you need

BBQ

6 tbsp BBQ sauce

½ tsp liquid smoke

Chilli

2 tbsp sriracha (or chilli sauce, see page 166)

1 tbsp soy sauce

1 tbsp maple syrup

Honey Soy

3 tbsp dark soy sauce

1 tbsp honey

1 tsp grated ginger

1 clove of garlic, minced

¼ tsp Chinese five spice

Pinch of black pepper

Mexican

2 tbsp olive oil

2 tbsp lime juice

1 tbsp honey

2 tsp chilli powder

1 tsp smoked paprika

½ tsp garlic powder

Here's how

1. Prepare the tofu or tempeh by removing it from the packet and wrapping the block in kitchen roll or a clean tea towel to absorb excess liquid. Slice or dice as required.
2. Combine all the ingredients for your chosen marinade in a sealable plastic bag. Add the prepared tofu or tempeh, then mix gently until coated.
3. Store the bag in the fridge to marinate from 15 minutes up to 2 or 3 days. These recipes are for roughly 1 block of tofu or tempeh. To marinate more, just scale up the quantities.

SERVES 2-4 | VEGAN

Veggie Crisps

Potato crisps are my weakness. I have taken these off my grocery list because each time I purchase them; they are eaten within the day – a whole family size pack! So now I tend to make my own, but only when I am craving them.

What you need

1 large sweet potato
1 large parsnip
1 large beetroot
1 large carrot
1-2 tbsp olive oil
Sea salt, to taste

Here's how

1. Preheat the oven to 180°c while you slice the veggies into thin rounds with a mandoline. Place them all into a large mixing bowl.
2. Toss the slices with the olive oil and a few sprinkles of sea salt, ensuring that each slice is coated and seasoned evenly.
3. Line a large baking tray with baking paper and lay the sliced veggies on it in a single layer. Bake for about 20 minutes in the preheated oven, flipping the rounds over after about 12 minutes. Keep an eye on them as they can burn quite quickly.
4. Remove the tray from the oven when the veggies look golden. Leave them to stand for 5 minutes before eating to allow them to cool and crisp up. Sprinkle with additional sea salt or any other seasoning of your choice and enjoy!

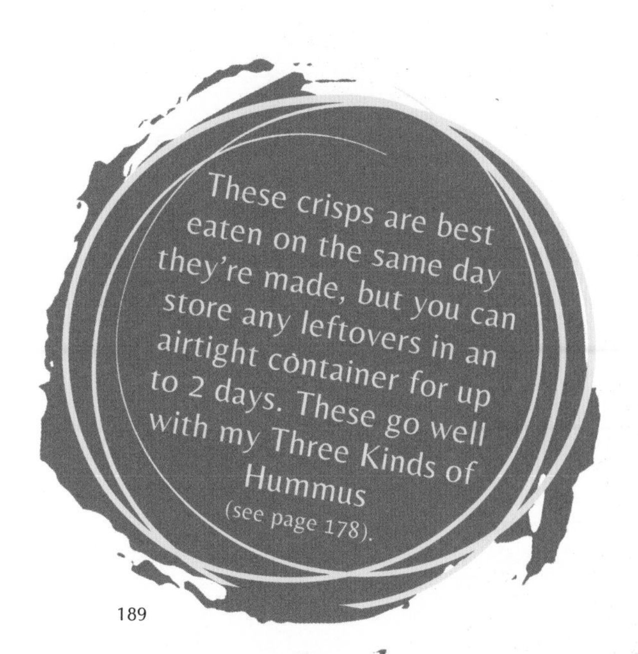

First edition printed in 2021 in the UK

ISBN: 978-1-910863-80-0

Written by: Jasmine Cassells

Edited by: Phil Turner &
Katie Fisher

Food Photography by: Paul Gregory

Portraits: Rob Hudson

Designed by: Paul Cocker
and Lucy Godbold
(godboldlucy.myportfolio.com)

PR: Emma Toogood/Lizzy Capps

Contributors: Lucy Anderson,
Suki Broad, Michael Johnson,
Alexander McCann, Lizzie Morton

Printed and bound in the UK by
Bell & Bain Ltd, Glasgow

Thank you to Club Backdrops

Published by Meze Publishing Limited

Unit 1b, 2 Kelham Square

Kelham Riverside

Sheffield S3 8SD

Web: www.mezepublishing.co.uk

Telephone: 0114 275 7709

Email: info@mezepublishing.co.uk